Looking at the Roots
A Guide to Understanding Orff Schulwerk

Wolfgang Hartmann

Printed in the U.S.A. No part of this publication may be reproduced, stored in a retrieval system or transmitted, in any form, by any means, electronic, mechanical, photocopying, recording, or otherwise, without the prior written permission of the Publisher: Pentatonic Press, 1232 Second Avenue, San Francisco, CA 94122.

For further information, go to: www.pentatonicpress.com

Cover Design: Lisa Berman
Editor: Carolee Stewart
Book design and typesetting: Bill Holab Music
ISBN 0-9773712-9-8

Cultivate the root; the leaves and branches
will take care of themselves.

—Confucius

Contents

Foreword

I don't remember precisely when I first met Wolfgang Hartmann, but I do remember that within five minutes, we were having a stimulating conversation about the philosophy of Orff Schulwerk, that dynamic approach to music education that had become the center of our professional lives. In the years that followed, our paths often crossed at Orff Schulwerk gatherings in Salzburg, Spain, San Francisco, and Helsinki and such conversations continued, often within a few minutes of seeing each other again. I found in Wolfgang a fellow fascination with the deep principles and ideas behind the practice, a relentless curiosity to know more and dig deeper, a commitment to lifting the ideas out of mere philosophy into the concrete world of playing, singing, and dancing with others.

I also had the good fortune to attend his workshops, which were filled with imaginative ways to create complex music from simple ideas. Modeling his own high level of musicality, he lifted the students up into improvisations and musical creations far beyond where they thought they could go. Always with warmth, care, humor, and a playful atmosphere that made each class memorable.

I learned so much from this thoughtful man. Whereas I was trained in the United States by people distant from the source of Carl Orff's Bavaria and his Orff Institute in Salzburg, Wolfgang studied at the Orff Institute, connected with the people who had worked with Carl Orff and Gunild Keetman. As a native Bavarian, he also intimately knew the historical and cultural context in which the Schulwerk developed and grew.

I remember one conversation in Spain suggesting he share his vast knowledge and experience with us in a book and discovered that he had already been thinking along those lines. It was a short step to suggesting that my Pentatonic Press publish it and many steps later, you hold it here in your hand.

Following the idea that you can only go as far forward as you can reach back, Wolfgang walks us through an informative and fascinating look back at the guiding principles of Orff Schulwerk and how they developed, always with the intent to use them to inform our practice today and move it yet further forward. Many contemporary Orff Schulwerk teachers are delighted by ideas and material in a workshop and hunger to try them out in Monday's classes. Yet, without that deep understanding of their source and depth of artistic vision, there is the danger of mere surface teaching, lowering a once vibrant, dynamic, and alive practice down to mere fun and cute activities. Wolfgang's book serves as a reminder to consider the essential pedagogical principles that will guide us to the kind of education that children—and artists of all ages—both need and deserve. Here is an opportunity to look back down the path to understand where we have been, how we arrived where we are, and what the next step may be.

Enjoy the walk!

Doug Goodkin

PREFACE

Orff Schulwerk is one of the most important concepts of music pedagogy worldwide. Since its beginnings nearly one hundred years ago and its first application in primary schools in 1948, it has lost nothing of its initial attractiveness. Just the contrary: it is alive more than ever. It is in practice all over the world in all possible pedagogical areas from kindergarten to grade school classrooms to helping seniors and people with disabilities.

Unfortunately, popularity also has a price: The pervasiveness of Orff Schulwerk has led in too many places to certain superficiality. The pedagogical base is not sufficiently known to every Orff practitioner, and as a consequence Orff's intention is occasionally turned into its opposite. In other words: Having children playing on xylophones does not guarantee that their playing is fostered by the energizing creativity that is a central feature of Orff Schulwerk.

This book offers information that gives insight into the music pedagogical work of Carl Orff and Gunild Keetman. Therefore, it describes the process of its origin and development as well as the objectives that the two authors wanted to achieve with it. The book tries to point out how Carl Orff was allowed to develop his own creativity in his childhood, and how this personal experience made him sure that children could create their own music.

It touches the difficulty of surviving as an artist during a perilous political time and gives space to describe the professional career of collaborator Gunild Keetman, who too often is forgotten or underestimated in her contribution to Orff Schulwerk. It points out that Orff Schulwerk emanates from the same philosophical and artistic spirit as Orff's operas and the famous *Carmina Burana*, and therefore it has to be seen as equal in the entirety of his oeuvre.

To put the intentions of the Schulwerk into praxis requires certain teaching qualities. The teacher has to be open in order to give the necessary room for creative contributions by the students, a sine qua non to calling the classroom activity an Orff Schulwerk lesson.

A special point of observation is cast on the relationship between Orff Schulwerk and instrumental education, a connection that is not free of conflicting questions. However, if the problematic topics are recognized and respected, Orff Schulwerk can enrich instrument teaching.

It has to be understood that teaching Orff Schulwerk is neither a plain technique nor a simple series of methodical steps but the result of a profound understanding of its artistic and pedagogical origin and dimension.

CHAPTER 1
A Small Start with Far-Reaching Repercussions

On the 15th of September in the year 1948 Radio München (now Bayerischer Rundfunk/Bavarian Radio) put a new program on the air. It was about music education for children in primary schools. The first edition was initially projected as a series of 14 programs titled *Das Orff-Schulwerk*. Although Carl Orff had already gained international fame as a composer, no one could have predicted what would follow from such an unpretentious and modest beginning. Who would have thought that a simple radio program for children in primary school would continue to echo further into the world?

In fact, the doubts were well-grounded. At that time Germany had more serious problems. Three years after the end of World War II, many cities were still in ruins and under mountains of debris. The country was occupied and administratively divided between the four victorious powers. The investigation into the full scope of the Nazi crimes had just begun. On top of that, only a few Bavarian schools had radios available in their classrooms. How could this new program series have mattered?

In addition to these adverse general conditions, the educational world also seemed to be reluctant. Walter Panofsky (1962), who gave the important impulse for this new program, reported on a conference of school directors that took place in Nuremberg during the summer of 1948. Representatives of the radio station presented the first recordings of this new program under the title "Education through Radio." The reaction—according to Panofsky—was not enthusiastic. As one participant commented, there was "…a whole series of pieces composed by Mozart when he was young, which was particularly suitable for introducing music to a child." It was suggested that it would be better to produce radio programs with classical music that would serve precisely the highest goal, "to arouse a timely appreciation of the music of the great masters" (Panofsky, 1962, p. 71). Was there really a need for something new? So was the opinion of the majority.

Luckily these reactions during the convention of school directors did not mirror the reactions of teachers after the first broadcasts. In fact, there was a sizable group of Bavarian teachers who welcomed these new programs enthusiastically. In addition, there came a strong impulse from outside Germany. Music pedagogues from different parts of the world—probably attracted by the name of the *Carmina Burana* composer Carl Orff—found interest in the programs within a short time. They discovered very soon that something completely new was being offered. Children were invited and inspired to make up their own music together with their classmates, with instruments that could be played immediately and without going through a tiring process of learning and practicing. They were able to make a music that understands dance as an integral part of musical expression and gives a central space to creativity through improvisation and composition. In short, children were from the beginning acting as musicians.

First recordings of the Schulwerk in the radio station, directed by Gunild Keetman (1948).
(Carl-Orff-Stiftung/Archiv: Orff-Zentrum München; Stiftung F.C. Gundlach)

More than seventy years have passed since the first release of the Schulwerk radio programs, but the basic idea of Orff's concept is as fresh and vital as it was on the first day. It keeps working and growing and evolving. Though the original Orff Schulwerk compositions by Carl Orff and Gunild Keetman are still worthy of enjoyment, they are no longer the exclusive center of the Schulwerk. Today it includes the cultural reality of every country where Schulwerk is taught, following accurately Carl Orff's advice,

> When you work with Schulwerk abroad, you must start all over again from the experience
> of the local children. And the experiences of children in Africa are different from those
> in Hamburg or Stralsund, and again from those in Paris or Tokyo. (Regner, 2011/1984,
> p. 220) [1]

However, new adoptions and additions also involve certain dangers. Not everything that happens with xylophones and the other Orff instruments in schools, workshops, and concerts has to do with the spirit and the objectives of Orff Schulwerk. Not all that is labeled with "Orff" contains Orff's initial spirit and vision. Already in 1962, we find Carl Orff complaining about questionable developments: "Mistaken interpretations and the nonsensical misuse of the instruments threatened in many places to turn the whole meaning of Schulwerk into the very opposite of what had been intended" (Orff, 2011b/1964, p. 150).

---

[1] A note about citations: Many of the works on the subject of Orff Schulwerk written in German by Carl Orff, Gunild Keetman, and others are now available in English translation. While the author consulted these works in the original language, the sources cited throughout this book are the translations because this book is aimed at English readers. In cases where there is an English translation, citations in the text will list first the date of the translated source, then the original date, and last, the page number(s) in the translated source.

How can Orff Schulwerk distance itself from these "dubious practices?" What does Orff Schulwerk mean today? What are its principal objectives and concerns? It is imperative to orient ourselves towards basic principles that define the core of the Schulwerk in a permanently changing world. This is the goal of this book: by looking back at its origins, to look forward and highlight what gives Orff Schulwerk its character. Knowing this, we can avoid the superficial interpretation of Orff and Keetman's depth of vision and consider how to move it forward.

Without going deeper into this aspect here, we will consider the following: Today Orff Schulwerk defines itself primarily as a particular way of teaching in the field of music and dance. There are two decisive points.

a) The musical material

Every teacher who is working in the concept of Orff Schulwerk has to choose the appropriate content (e.g., song, dance piece of music, speech piece, story, visual starting point like graphic notation, picture). But this freedom to choose includes responsibility. The teacher's choices should adhere to a certain criterion of quality. A look to the first Orff Schulwerk volumes shows that, in this original material by Orff and Keetman, no tasteless and falsely idyllic songs and texts can be found. It is just the contrary if we think of the harsh texts with a clear reference to the Thirty Years' War. (See Chapter 7.)

b) The teaching process

The crucial part is the teaching process itself, i.e., what methodical steps are taken to influence the direction of the work in the classroom. These decisions are entirely in the hands of the teacher. Ultimately, that process will prove if it can count as an "Orff Schulwerk class." The students may dance and play Orff instruments, but that does not in and of itself qualify their experience as Orff Schulwerk. If there is no space for ideas and contributions to come from the students, no suggestion that finds its place in the final result—in other words, only the exact planning of the teacher is realized (his or her compositions, arrangements, and dance instructions)—then it cannot be labeled as "Orff Schulwerk."

Consequently, the Schulwerk as an open way of teaching needs a teacher's profile that is able to serve these demands. Someone who needs an exactly worked-out teaching 'script' that comes as fast as possible to a presentable result may not find pleasure in the Schulwerk. But music pedagogues who are open for experiments and teachers who take the creative potential of their students seriously will find abundant stimulations in Orff and Keetman's concept.

This is why, from the beginning, it has been stressed that Orff Schulwerk is not a method, not a formula to be applied unconsciously, nor a recipe to be mechanically followed. It needs the teacher's right attitude and pedagogical philosophy.

There has to be a clear and deep understanding of "the roots," i.e., the philosophy of the Orff Schulwerk. What is it about? What were the fundamental intentions behind the creation of this concept? Also very important: "Do I agree with this thinking? Can I find myself in this artistic pedagogical concept?" And what are—if we stay in this image of a tree—"the different branches?" What are the main objectives, the teaching principles, and tools of expression that are used? Having established a pedagogical foundation in this way, teachers will be able to realize their teaching successfully with the appropriate methodical steps and creative impulses. In addition to the professional competences indisputably required in the field of music and dance, the Schulwerk sets itself apart by focusing on the personal qualities of the teacher. (See Chapter 8.)

These qualities that the Orff Schulwerk requires include:

• **Confidence in the students**
A firm belief in the imagination, inventiveness, and creative potential of one's students as an essential starting—and ending—point.

• **Tolerance for ambiguity**
The process of creating needs time and patience. One must not be content with rapidly found solutions. It is necessary to leave the process of deciding open for a certain time in order to allow alternative options.

• **Social competence and responsibility**
Creative processes ask for decisions. When we decide among different options, some ideas will necessarily be dropped. This can create disappointment and the teacher has to take the emotional consequences, especially when dealing with children or adolescents. The group dynamic has to be observed and, if necessary, positively influenced. Rivalry and competitive thinking may destroy the classroom atmosphere and hinder creative processes.

Respecting and following these "rules of the game" opens the door to a wide field of music and movement education that will be enriching and satisfying for both the student and the teacher.

CHAPTER 2
Living in the Schulwerk–Echoes of Carl Orff's Childhood and Youth

Did Carl Orff in 1948 become a pedagogue by working on the Schulwerk for the radio programs? Surely not. He had already been teaching in the Günther-Schule in 1924. But what was new in 1948 was that the program was directed to children, not to adult students. The Günther-Schule in Munich (1924-1944) was an educational institution for gymnastics, music, and dance and the students were young adults completing their professional training. Carl Orff gave inspiration for their further artistic and pedagogical development based on his musical and creative expertise. This cooperative work with school founder Dorothee Günther gave feet to his emerging vision, allowing him to put his ideas about music and dance expression into practice. In so doing, a new and original musical style emerged, something based on a different premise than the art music of the times.

Orff called it *Elementare Musik*—Elemental Music. It was a music that invites all to participate and includes dance as an important component. Stated more precisely in his own words:

> *Elemental music is never music alone but forms a unity with movement, dance, and speech. It is music that one makes oneself, in which one takes part not as a listener but as a participant. It is unsophisticated, employs no big forms and no big architectural structures, and it uses small sequence forms, ostinato, and rondo. Elemental music is near to the earth, natural, physical, within the range of everyone to learn it and to experience it, and suitable for the child.* (Orff, 2011b/1964, p. 144)

Closely connected was the development of a set of instruments appropriate to this purpose.

Someone who wants to understand the terminology of Orff Schulwerk has to draw a clear line between "elementary" and "elemental." While elementary refers to the simple, the basic, the starting steps of entering an area that will become more complicated, elemental has a slightly different meaning. One feels the depth of the term in expressions like "elemental forces" or "elemental needs," which have nothing to do with simple or easy. Because the German equivalent *elementar* does not distinguish between elementary and elemental, Carl Orff repeatedly felt impelled to explain what he meant with *das Elementare*. "The elemental always means a new beginning...In its timelessness the elemental finds understanding all over the world...The elemental is always reproductive" (Orff, 1978/1976, p. 277).

The experience in the Günther-Schule allowed him also to reflect about musical activities for non-professionals and children (*Laien und Kinder*). In Orff's essays and speeches during the 1930s we find statements like the following:

> *Musical instruction for a child does not begin in the music lesson. Playtime is the starting point. One should not come to music—it should arise of itself. What is important is that the child be allowed to play, undisturbed.* (Orff, 2011a/1932, p. 68)

In addition to all the experience that he gained in the Günther-Schule, there was another treasure of experience to which he could refer: It was likely that he was thinking back to his own early childhood, when he himself could experience what it meant "to play, undisturbed." It was a time of security in the family, a time when he could enter the world of sounds, tones, and rhythms in a playful way.

Carl Orff (1898).
Carl-Orff-Stiftung/Archiv: Orff-Zentrum München

The memories of these early experiences provided him the best proof for his recommendation to let children play by following their own intentions and intuitions. The written records that his grandfather kept from Carl's earliest days surely were fostering his memories. According to this chronicle, Carl was not yet three when he wanted to explore his mother's piano on his own: "I gathered complex sounds with both hands, which I repeated again and again, loudly and softly" (Orff, 1975a, p. 21). Quite soon other instruments were discovered as there were drum, glockenspiel, and mouth organ. His grandfather took note: "He played on the mouth organ the story of an ill child and his recovery" (p. 22).

In 1932, more than thirty years later, having these memories in his mind, Orff wrote about the musical development of a child: "…finding something new, discovering for oneself. This is the decisive factor, not the imitation and reproduction of others' ideas" (Orff, 2011a/1932, p. 74).

The first of the eight volumes of his *Dokumentation* (published between 1975 and 1983)— about his childhood—is full of examples of how Carl Orff dealt with his world around him, inventing and discovering the music. Ulrike E. Jungmair (1992, p. 69) expresses an interesting assumption: "The underlying intention in his reminiscences to make basics of his elemental music and movement education evident, especially … the unity of music, movement, and speech…is highly visible." And, leaving aside Orff's musical talent and extraordinary receptivity and learning aptitude, "Orff's memories make in many ways visible elemental capabilities and skills as they are characteristic for all children of average talent."

Not yet ten, he spotted in his grandfather's attic the stand of a puppet theater. The puppets had disappeared, which did not bother him at all. He made his own new ones, along with the scenery. And, of course, the stage play itself. "One of my first plays could have been almost called an improvised opera; it was named *In the Magic Forest*" (Orff, 1975a, p. 280). The music included a glockenspiel, tremolos on the piano, sounds on the zither, and a box with peas and chestnuts as a shaker. Even visual special effects were not missed, including fireworks and smoke. It is not surprising that his mother felt quite worried. After the first performance she asked Carl to not use so much magic in the future and to keep a filled bucket of water within reach.

This attitude of doing things in his own way was not limited to musical activities. When he came to secondary school, he started to write a "Romantic Botany," where he described in a poetic way flowers according to their appearance in the sequence of the seasons. The biologic systematization of gymnosperm and angiosperm plants—as it was presented in school—was too boring for him.

In this example we see the conflict between the exciting discovering-on-his-own and direct implementation in praxis on one hand, and the theory-oriented didactic systematic thinking that limited his creative explorations on the other. This difficult relationship between creative liberty and formal constraints runs like a thread through his childhood and this period of his education. The first piano lessons with his mother were received as something new and exciting, but soon came the finger exercises, which did not excite him at all (Orff, 1975a, p. 280). The fact that he as a child liked reading and writing music may be surprising on the first view, because these activities go beyond not only music making, but also include theoretical knowledge. But little Carl sensed instinctively that the ability to write music opened further opportunities to find his own music. Echoing in his pedagogical vision his own rich experiences as a child, he would later help many other children to be their own composers.

During his years in secondary school Carl Orff experienced the same dualism between personal vision and the formal reality of a school system. He felt the education system to be an obstacle rather than a help for his future development. "The time at the secondary school… became almost a torment, as it held me off principally from what I wanted to do and from what I believed I had to do" (Orff, 1975a, p. 280). The school achievements became worse and worse (with the exception of Latin) and consequently he dropped out just short of taking the final exam (*Abitur*). It was a considerable scandal in a family where university education was an unwritten requirement. But he felt free now to concentrate on studies in music.

But the next disappointment was not far away. The *Musikakademie* in Munich did not fulfill his expectations. Again, he encountered the tension between his personal aspirations and the inflexible institutional structures: "The whole Academy was conservative and patriarchal. I had lived my own different ideas, plans, and experiments in the wild too long to reinsert myself into the narrowness of this institute" (Orff, 1975a, p. 280). Consequently, he began looking for private teachers also "in the wild."

At that time, World War I was raging, and Orff was drafted into the army. It proved to be but a short interruption in his studies because he was seriously injured during his first mission and was sent home.

Fast forward now to the autumn of 1921. As he himself explained, Orff wanted to "learn, learn, learn." He engaged in self-study with the "old masters" (Claudio Monteverdi, Heinrich Schütz, and others). And he tells us, "I tried to gain knowledge and experience, and I let others participate in this attempt in order to gain clarity—I started to teach" (Orff (1975) quoted in Jans, 1996, p. 73). Rarely do we find so clearly expressed how Carl Orff wanted to resolve this often-experienced dualism: combining "the studying teacher" with "the teaching student" in one person. This attitude describes so straightforwardly Orff's vision of a teacher. He does not stay face to face in front of the students, but he looks in the same direction. He goes the same way, but ahead as the educator. In a remarkable way Orff's understanding of being an educator goes straight back to the linguistic roots of the word: *dux* [Lat.] i.e., the duke, the one who leads by going ahead. The teacher is the one who is believed to know the way and shows the way, but he also is a seeker. There is no space for a tight didactic system. It is the creative intuition and awareness of responsibility that define the guiding "teacher-student."

This point of view may help us to understand Orff's aversion to theorizing his Schulwerk. In this he was quite radical. "Didactic" was one of his central words of contempt! The "Schulwerk" was the Schulwerk, no more explanation and theory were necessary. I remember a conversation with Liselotte, Carl Orff's widow. The subject was about the current development of the Schulwerk, about its international expansion and the addition of new musical materials. When I used the expression "pedagogy of the Schulwerk" to refer to the way of teaching Schulwerk independent from the material used, she literally winced and said, "'Pedagogy of the Schulwerk'—if Orff would hear that!"

Further to this point, during the 1985 Symposium in Salzburg, where international teachers of the Schulwerk gathered, Werner Thomas expressed it this way: "Orff could never come to terms with the theories of methodology and didactics. He had conceived his Schulwerk through and through from the elemental nature of a child's world and according to artistic standards and aims" (Thomas, 1985, p. 29).

If we review Orff's musical evolution, his joy of discovery and creativity as a child, his way to his own music, feeling all systematic teaching structures as impediments, we understand why he was trying—in both his composition and also in his Schulwerk—to find the direct way to music through one's own experience instead of through theoretical systematizing. Consequently, there are very few methodical hints in the five central volumes of *Orff-Schulwerk–Music for Children*. Orff did not want to explain too much; he was convinced that the Schulwerk was explaining itself. Repeating how Liselotte Orff expressed it: "For him the Schulwerk was the 'Schulwerk;' no need for further explanations." Certainly, this made sense in the first years after 1948, as long as the teachers could listen to the Schulwerk programs on the radio.

But lacking the clarity that was provided by the programs on the radio and later on television, many teachers felt left alone. They only had available the scores that were used in the radio programs. Too many questions and doubts remained unanswered and caused frequent misinterpretations. The collection of material in the books did not give any methodical help because it was following musical criteria. The first volume is limited to the pentatonic scale and simple rhythmic patterns; Volumes II and III contain songs and pieces in major scales; Volumes IV and V include pieces in modes and minor scales. The fact, however, that the first volume begins with very basic and simple melodies in 2- and 3-tone ranges, and the last volume (V) includes compositions that contain literary and philosophical content far beyond the range of elementary school does not mean that these resources can be interpreted as a practical didactic guide. Orff was thinking in a completely natural way. He knew "as a child" how it starts (or better, how it should start) and as an adult he illustrated how his elemental music revealed an artistic and philosophical depth and perspective clearly separated from the so-called art music. Therefore again: The original printed materials of the Schulwerk are just an offering to the teacher. They are presented in a way that the teacher has to know which of the different pieces are appropriate in the classroom.

When Carl Orff received the invitation in 1948 to create a radio program for music education in primary school, he felt it more as an inconvenience than as a welcome opportunity. He had turned his professional attention completely to the theater and was working on his opera *Antigonae*. He considered his music pedagogical work to be finished, probably with a drop of bitterness in his mind. Previously, during the early 1930s there had been intentions to implement Orff's Schulwerk into the regular school system. Leo Kestenberg, consultant for music pedagogy at the Prussian Ministry of Culture in Berlin, had shown great interest in Orff's *Elementare Musikerziehung*. Kestenberg worked on a reorganization of music education and saw an opportunity to integrate Orff's concept into the curriculum. But all plans to put these ideas into practice were frustrated by the political developments in Germany. Leo Kestenberg had to leave the country and his plans were stopped (Orff, 1964, p. 15).

And so, Orff's decision to accept the radio program offer came quite reluctantly. Walter Panofsky tells us:

> *He obviously did not find it easy to start again from the beginning...He still regarded the whole thing as an experiment whose results were uncertain: he almost appeared to be more concerned in proving its validity to himself rather than to the world in general.* (Panofsky, 1962, p. 71)

Together with his former student and later colleague Gunild Keetman and Rudolf Kirmeyer,[1] the designated presenter of the new series, Orff started to develop concepts for the programs. He recognized more and more the opportunity of the radio as a medium to realize his music pedagogical visions. Without the need to deal with school-didactic obligations, he could bring the Schulwerk "from outside" into the classroom. It allowed to Orff that his Schulwerk never became a schoolbook. Hermann Regner, former director of the Orff Institute in Salzburg, expressed it like this: "The Schulwerk volumes never were modern, so they never became out-of-fashion." [2]

The difficult relationship between vision and institutional reality that Carl Orff had experienced so often during earlier years came again to the surface. When he talked of his academy studies and said that it was impossible to reinsert himself "into the narrowness of this institute," we only have to replace "institute" with "school authority" to imagine his concern that the "wild experiment of the Schulwerk" would be reduced to a "domestic house plant" in the school.

But the conflict could be avoided. The Bavarian Radio could provide him a safe distance from the didactic reality of the classroom. The task to implement the Schulwerk into the daily work in the classroom was given over to the individual teacher in the school. It allowed Orff and Keetman's legacy to be kept as an uncontaminated source.

---

1 Rudolf Kirmeyer was director of a Public School in Munich, well-known for his music programs on the radio.
2 Personal notes from a lecture at the Orff-Institute, 1975–1977.

CHAPTER 3

Carmina Burana—The Schulwerk—The Theater
"The Tripartite Orff"

The tripartite Orff. A composer has seldom made it so easy to be put into three clearly separated and different categories:

1. There is first of all the "*Carmina Burana* Orff," composer of one of the world's most popular
   choral works.
2. Then Orff, the initiator of the Schulwerk who has made an enormous impact on music
   education worldwide.
3. Finally, Carl Orff, the composer of numerous, successfully performed operas and stage
   works.

We can assume that he would have become famous even if he had limited himself to only one
of these three branches. So, it is no surprise that a great number of his admirers who confine
themselves exclusively to one of these three areas ignore too often the importance of the other
two by giving preference to their own favorite category. It is obviously not necessary for them
to look for connecting aspects to the other branches of Orff's work, as they enjoy and admire
their personal segment of Orff's contribution.

Carmina Burana fans can find a performance scheduled at almost any time somewhere in the
world, presented by groups ranging from professional companies to amateur choirs, church and
school choirs. Some are large spectacles, complete with full orchestra, choir, and *con imaginibus
magicis*, as Orff subtitled the choreographic performance. Other performances are more modest, without dance, and with only two pianos and percussion, which is also officially authorized
by Carl Orff. The inherent rhythmic drive, the strictly maintained strophic form in many parts,
and catchy melodies all help *Carmina Burana* feel accessible to people who normally do not
listen to classical music. The fact that distinct quotations of the composition, especially from
the opening part, appear in commercials, and the fact that adaptations of the *Carmina* can be
heard in rock concerts prove the special hit character of this composition. It has achieved an
exceptional position in the musical oeuvre of the 20th century. If there is a "one-hit-wonder"
equivalent in classical music, Orff and *Carmina Burana* would qualify.

Then there are the "Schulwerk people." Many of them see Carl Orff almost exclusively as the
founder of a music pedagogical concept. As the Orff Schulwerk receives continuously growing
attention worldwide, it may even happen that "Orff" stands in some countries as a synonym
for any type of early childhood music education.

While *Carmina Burana* with its worldwide success appears more as a curiosity and peculiar
coincidence, Orff's creative work for the theater, by comparison, is very often not even noticed.
The "theater people" have yet a different point of view. Orff's commitment to pedagogical
issues seems for many of them more of an incomprehensible and even dispensable lapse. They
draw a clear line between "artistic" and "pedagogic" Orff. Liselotte Orff told me during an

interview for a radio program, "The theater people always said: 'Orff, leave this pedagogic stuff away, write more for the theater! But when he got angry because a new stage production did not conform to his imagination, then he was even more pleased how heartily he was received and appreciated in the 'Orff Schulwerk world.'"

So here we have the picture of the "tripartite Orff:" the perception of an outstanding artistic personality seen from three completely different perspectives.

Of course, we know that this classification is over simplified and more than questionable. Werner Thomas, Orff's erudite companion, advisor, and also commentator on his works, offered a different point of view. He pointed out that Orff's theater compositions and his pedagogical work have to be seen as an intellectual unity. "His tonal thinking allowed him to move back and forth between large form and cellular unit without rank degradation" and cannot be isolated (Thomas, 1986, no page numbers). It is worthwhile to follow this statement and look for the connecting threads between the different parts of Orff's creative activities.

Some facts are evident and easily to find. One can hardly miss the stylistic similarity between *Carmina Burana* and the Schulwerk. In both, we find the development of Orff's style of elemental music. Orff compared his Schulwerk to a quarry from which he could take construction blocks (i.e., musical motives) for *Carmina Burana* and others of his later works. Likewise, his compositional approach in these works found its way into *Music for Children* compositions that both he and Keetman wrote in a simpler form. The composer and the pedagogue were two sides of the same artist.

In short, the general concept of the Schulwerk breathes the spirit of a composer (really, of two composers—not to forget the co-genius of Gunild Keetman). Even if the compositions of the Schulwerk (songs and other pieces) have to be seen only as models to stimulate creative processes in the students, the beauty and authentic power of these musical miniatures cannot be ignored. The Schulwerk does not deal with learning and practicing but it always aims toward a well finished result, an artistic final entity, the ending of a creative process. The fact that this product can be quite simple according to the age and development of the students does not detract from its authenticity and aesthetic-artistic content.

But someone may also see a contradiction between these labels of "Pedagogic Orff" and "Composer Orff." Pedagogy is forward looking; it intends to foster moral concepts and models of behavior that should be valid in the future. On the compositional side, we recognize in so many places Orff's focus on the past, his regard for historic periods. We only have to look at all the historic topics he brought to the stage—the ancient Greek story of *Antigonae*, the medieval material of *Carmina Burana*, the old German folk tales of *Der Mond* and *Die Kluge*. Orff's interest in the past runs like a thread throughout his creative work.

Orff's interest in the past is more than an expedition into a remote and unknown area. It is rather a familiarity with rediscovering and finding home. He describes his first encounter with Monteverdi's *Orfeo* score as follows:

> *I found music that was as familiar to me as I had known it for a long time, as if I just had found it again. It was a concordance that moved me and opened space for something new... Here were new ground plans, here still was everything burgeoning and open for every development; here was the beginning that I was looking for... Here I hoped to sense a new way to the music on the stage, a way that could help me along. I wanted to start ab ovo.*[1] (Orff (1975) quoted in Jans, 1996, pp. 75–76)

---

1   ...from the beginning, the origin, the egg.

We have to interpret carefully this interest in the past. Orff's devotion to history is never historicizing or museum-like. On the contrary, he sees first of all what has a timeless value. In *Carmina Burana* we observe that Orff did not focus on historical aspects. He ignored the medieval music notation and liberated the power of rhythm that he sensed in the words. It was not the reconstruction that motivated Orff, but the new definition of inspiration. He was looking for elements from history that were still vivid, that still had a value that deserved to come to life again in his stage works.

When Orff was looking for "the new," he did it by looking to the past, to the origins that might have been buried over the course of time. One may compare Orff to an architect who does not construct his buildings on grid squares but unearths old foundations to use them for his new structures. It is the respect for that which already existed. The evidence is manifold: During his studies while composing *Antigonae*, Orff discovered that he could "sense, set free, and redesign the music that is already contained in Hölderlin's text" (Orff, quoted in Jans, 1996, p. 155). In 1977, he said to Werner Thomas, on the occasion of setting poems of Catull to music: "Yes, Catull has already composed it. I only have written it down" (Thomas, 1990 p. 181).

Where were the origins? How did it start? Orff's radical idea was to hark back to the beginnings of things to find his way forward. In 1921, just 26 years old, he began to study the *Alte Meister* with a main focus on Renaissance music. With his study of Monteverdi, he came to the beginnings of European opera. The beginnings of European music theater he found later in the Greek tragedies.

Is it really surprising that Orff was asking how music starts for the human being? Surely Orff remembered his first experience with music, and this brought him to lullabies, finger plays, and nursery rhymes. Even more extreme, the next question: Where does music start to be music? Here we come to shepherds' calls, market shouts, and melodic tale-telling—bridges between spoken words and the origins of music. And thus arrives the concept of the Schulwerk. The view backward becomes meaningful for the future and any contradiction is dissolved.

The intellectual unity of Orff's theater repertoire and his pedagogical work is based on this sensitivity for the organically grown. In both, he bases his concepts on that which already exists. In the Schulwerk he uses on one hand the rich resources of popular rhymes, dance games, and riddles. On the other hand, even more important, he trusts the creative potential inherent in every child. It is the foundation of his music pedagogic vision: encouraging children to trust in their own creative power.

The tripartite Orff? We can conclude that there are not only strong lines of connection between the different branches of Carl Orff's body of work, but also that the work consists essentially of different facets of the same vision. Based on Werner Thomas' assertions (Thomas, 1986), we can assume that the inner logic and philosophical consistency allowed him to be equally convincing in the artistic world of the theater as well as in the field of pedagogy.

In the end, there are not "three Orffs" but only one.

CHAPTER 4
Working in a Difficult Time

The period of National Socialism in Germany between 1933 and 1945 was a grim time to be alive. Orff lived through this time of the Third Reich as a composer who had his music performed. Precisely his most famous work, *Carmina Burana*, which finally gave him worldwide fame, was brought on stage in Germany during the year 1937. At that time, the Nazis had been in power for four years and had already abrogated the former democracy.

Everyone has seen in documentaries the marching masses on the Nuremberg rallies, the hysterically cheering crowds—and after the war the shocking pictures of mountains of dead bodies in the concentration camps. With the Holocaust, Germany had fallen into a moral abyss. This was a great blow to a culture that had brought forth the likes of Kant, Hegel, and Humboldt. After the collapse, there was a general awakening, shock, dismay, and astonishment that all this could have happened. Still, I remember the words of my history teacher in the post war time: "If you think you have to be proud of Goethe and Beethoven, you also have to be ashamed of Hitler and Himmler."

Of course, there appear questions. How could one survive as a known artist at such a time without being demonstratively in favor of, or if not, being suspected of opposing the regime? After all, Orff was able to work and have his music performed—a remarkable privilege during such a difficult time.

Carl Orff did not comment on this time publicly. In his *Dokumentation* (Orff, 1975–1984) we find only detailed biographic information about his childhood, his student days, and first employments, followed by the first years of the Schulwerk. In general, his compositions are the focus of his memoirs, with comments about their development and first performances. Time-related explanations appear only in incidental notes, e.g., "Plans to bring *Die Kluge* to the Berliner Staatsoper stage were lost in the disturbances of the years of war" (Orff, quoted in Jans, 1996, p. 140), or in reference to a newly revised version of his music to Shakespeare's *Midsummer Night's Dream* in the year 1944: "the circumstances at that time were not favorable for a performance and so it was put aside" (Jans, p. 135).

Indeed, the last years of the Second World War were more than just "not favorable." This quite mild expression can only be understood from the point of an artist who saw his creative work as the first and only mission in his life. He wanted to keep his world of art separate, not to be disturbed by the outside world.

Questions about Orff's political standing came out unexpectedly in 1995, the centenary of his birth. Suddenly, Orff's life during that time was being discussed publicly. In a British television documentary,[1] there appeared a mix of marching SS boots and bodies in concentration camps with underlying music from *Carmina Burana*. Almost simultaneously, Michael Kater (1995) published an article about "Carl Orff in the Third Reich." The world was shocked by

---

1 "O, Fortuna," London Weekend Television, 28 January 1995 (with a slightly softened version on German television) in Maier, 1995.

Kater's claims that Orff was a Nazi collaborator, and surely some readers may have found that it proved "what they always had suspected…" (Maier, 1995, p. 1).

Apart from the momentary confusion, it also had a positive consequence. Once publicly unwrapped, many began to look more closely at these issues. Several responses followed Kater's publication that treated the question of Carl Orff's connection with the potentates of the Third Reich in a more factual way. They did not discover much that was shockingly revealing, at least nothing that would prove an ideological and political closeness between Carl Orff and the regime (Thomas, 1995; Kugler, 2000; Regner, 1994; Maier, 1995).

Carl Orff's life (1895–1982) spanned four very different eras in German history. His childhood and youth took place during the *Kaiserzeit*, which in Bavaria was the Prince Regent Era, a period of great cultural and artistic importance. This period ended with the First World War. Then followed the time of the Weimar Republic between 1919 and 1933, with its cultural revolutionary tendencies (for example, the *Bauhaus*). This was also the period of the Günther-Schule. Then came the Hitler dictatorship, followed in 1945 by the reconstruction of democracy in the Federal Republic with its capital in Bonn.

Carl Orff did not comment on any of these distinctly different political periods in a specific or general way. Therefore, we cannot say that he disavowed the Nazi time. The fact that *Carmina Burana* premiered during the Third Reich does not make it "a child of that time." It was much more a late consequence of the development of his elemental music, which was connected with his time at the Günther-Schule. For him, it was a milestone on his way to realizing his personal style of composing. The difficulties and rejections that preceded the premiere of *Carmina* showed clearly that this work was not at all in the interest of the Nazi government. It was absolutely unwelcomed. On the other hand, the Nazis did not dare to just ban it.

What seems clear is that Orff did not look for any closeness to the Nazis, but neither did he act against them. Because he did not show any political profile, he was not so easily assailable. But the designation of Carl Orff's music as "Bavarian Nigger Music" by Hans Drewes (Kater, 1995, p. 11), the music assistant of *Reichspropagandaminister* Goebbels, shows in a drastic way that important parts of the high political ranks saw Orff's compositional style as non-desirable.

Also his (and Gunild Keetman's) contribution to the opening music of the 1936 Olympic Games in Berlin cannot be taken as support for the Nazi regime. In the political context, it was an event that can be seen as a last effort by many nations in the world to keep Hitler's Germany in the international community of civilized countries. At that sporting event, "even the later war enemies were sitting at Hitler's feet" (Maier, 1995, p. 9). Orff describes this event in his *Dokumentation*, Vol. III in this way:

> *Only when Diem*[1] *assured me that the Festival was an international Olympic occasion that allowed no kind of political bias, did I agree to his request and only then if the contract came directly from the Olympic Committee.* (Orff, 1978/1976, p. 205)

Nevertheless, the Olympic Games of 1936 had an enormous propagandist value for Hitler. What Carl Orff viewed from an artistic angle was welcomed by the Nazis as political success. Whether Orff did not see that or just accepted it remains unclear. Minna Ronnefeld, a later proponent of Orff Schulwerk, commented:

> *That Orff was stimulated by the idea of introducing his Schulwerk to an international audience is understandable; but it is surprising that at the same time he failed to realize*

---

1   Carl Diem was the general director and organizer of the 1936 Olympic Games in Berlin.

that his involvement could be interpreted as a sign of acceptance or also as indifference in relation to the Nazi regime. (Ronnefeld, 2013/2002, pp. 88–89)

This ambiguous point of view between artistic demand and political exploitation became even more obvious in another case. The race-based law of the national socialists decreed that all Non-Aryan creative artists—past or present—had to be excluded from the public cultural life, banned from performance, or hushed up. Among many others, Felix Mendelssohn-Bartholdy as "Jew Mendelssohn" fell victim to this law. But because his popular music seemed to be inseparably connected with Shakespeare's *Midsummer Night's Dream*, National Socialist cultural leaders were looking for an alternative music of high quality. Musicologist and music journalist Fred Prieberg noted that the Nazis already were trying to find a substitute for Mendelssohn-Bartholdy's music as early as 1934. Prieberg counts more than 40 attempts (Rösch, 2009, p. 51). Whereas other composers like Richard Strauss and Hans Pfitzner rejected the assignment, Orff accepted. Commenting on Orff's decision, Hans Maier later wrote: "This appears for us today as a bad kowtow to the most powerful representatives of that time" (Maier, 1995, p. 9).

Was Orff aware of the reason for composing new music to *Midsummer Night's Dream*? Did he pause to think that accepting the commission would be a form of endorsing this race-based law? Because Orff didn't comment directly on this, we are left to guess. What we do know is that Orff had thought about writing his own music to this Shakespearean play as early as 1917. Within the time span of nearly 50 years[!], he had created six different versions (the last in 1963). He felt Mendelssohn-Bartholdy's music was too soft, too sweet, too close to opera, and missed the very heart of Shakespeare's poetry (Orff, quoted in Jans, 1996, p. 133). In his opinion, his own musical imagination came closer to the content of the theater piece. When Orff was invited in 1938 to write his own music, he viewed it simply as a new opportunity to pursue a long existing objective.

But in the process of writing for the version presented in 1939, he had to agree to some concessions and the outcome was disappointing. Especially distressing for him was the fact that those who had expressed themselves negatively about his previous (and more vanguard) versions were now in praise of the actual adaption (Orff, quoted in Jans, 1996, p. 135).

So the question remains: How close was Carl Orff in fact to the Nazi regime? Even Michael Kater, who tried in his investigations again and again to situate Orff close to the political powers ("certain aspects of his style, which harmonized accidentally with the national-socialistic music aesthetic") had to admit "that this music after 1933 was a logical continuation of his work before Hitler's accession to power" and, Kater continues,

One has to conclude that under other political circumstances, for example in a democratic-republican system, he would not have composed differently from the way he did between 1933 and 1945. Then he could have dedicated himself deliberately and lightheartedly to a new musical version of the Midsummer Night's Dream in a non-anti-Semitic atmosphere. Hence Orff had not subordinated his composing style to any NS-requirements, nor had he ever intentionally embroidered his work with textual NS-elements. (Kater, 1995, p. 32)

It has to be put on record: Orff simply had no ideological or political relationship with the ruling powers. Certainly, he had to negotiate with different government cultural entities to allow presentations of his works. That he never could feel secure in that time can also be seen in a letter from his publisher Ludwig Strecker dated 13 July 1938. In the letter, Strecker wondered whether they could risk giving the premiere of *Der Mond* in Frankfurt:

> *Before we take this significant decision, I have to remind you again of the risks that are connected with this step. Your adversary is Gerigk, having the support of the Völkischer Beobachter.[1] It is quite sure that the Propaganda Ministry will join. It has to be taken into account that the Orff case will enter in a decisive phase. These people have a hundred means to destroy you completely, if they want to do so; you do not even need to compose Die Kluge or have further hopes. I do not want to say that this will happen, I only have to inform you seriously about that danger.* (Thomas, 1995).

Orff was more tolerated than accepted by some officials, as shown in an official comment by an NSDAP authority in 1942,

> *As composer he is acquiring ever more prominence and is praised in precisely those circles which are still today to be considered ideologically hostile. In our office there are doubts of an ideological kind about the "Musik-Schulwerk" produced by him, and we disassociate ourselves from his musical compositions. (Kugler, 2013a/2002, p. 19)*

His opera *Der Mond* [The Moon] (1939) and also *Die Kluge* [The Peasant's Wise Daughter] (1943) did not receive official approval, especially when the imprisoned father sings, "…and one who has the power, has the law, and who has the law, he also will bend it, because above everything rules violence." Also, the brazen words of the three rascals may not have been heard with delight when they sang, e.g., *"Fides ist geschlagen tot, Justitia lebt in grosser Not"* [fidelity is beaten to death, justice lives in deep misery] (Orff, 1943). Some benevolent person may see it almost as an allusion to the political situation of that time, a type of latent resistance. Hans Maier:

> *I fear that Orff has seen the politics at every time of his life under this light. It may not have been always as tyrannical and criminal as in the Third Reich. But politics could anyway dangerously distract and disturb someone who wanted to create and produce … The tyranny was for Orff first of all bad and evil, because it destroyed the personal realm of the art, as it was tearing everything into the maelstrom of politics.* (Maier, 1995, p. 10)

In contrast to all the frenetically cheering crowds in the propaganda films, it should be stated that a great part of the German population was quite soon tired and fed up with the Nazi regime. But to comment on this publicly was a life-threatening act. The police maintained a feared system of informants, and the approaching war made every remark potentially to be considered as high treason. Many simply hoped that the curse of the *Tausendjähriges Reich* would soon be over. It is most definitely not a simplification to count Carl Orff in this part of the population—neither affirming nor denying his politics. Hans Maier:

> *Even as he despised the Nazis from his heart, certainly he was no resistance fighter. But who can, who is allowed – above all someone born at a later time – to demand this so easily from an artist in the Third Reich?* (Maier, p. 11)

Orff's spontaneous reaction when he heard that his friend Kurt Huber (an active member of the resistance group *Weisse Rose*) was arrested, indeed can be seen as an instantaneous human debility. Huber's wife said that when she informed Carl Orff about the precarious situation of her husband, he did not show the expected empathy (Maier, p. 10). He saw himself in danger

---

1 Newspaper of the National Socialist German Workers Party

and was only reflecting the consequences for his compositional work. Like most other German citizens, Carl Orff went through a difficult time. It was a personal challenge, and he could not always evade contact with the political reality. What compromises had to be agreed to and which ones could have been avoided, is difficult to decide when seen from a later time. This is left to everyone's opinion.

In conclusion, as stated at the beginning of this chapter, Carl Orff lived through four very different times—four eras that could not be more diverse, with no transition time between two of them. From that perspective it is not farfetched to ask the questions: What is it that continues through all these changes? What keeps its value throughout the flow of time? What remains timeless? These are questions that appear again and again in the whole oeuvre of Carl Orff.

Franz Willnauer calls Orff's *Astutuli* a [time] "remote and timeless comedy" (Jans, 1986, p. 185). It is really "timeless" because the main theme of the plot is the vulnerability of the human being to manipulation. But the passing of time is also addressed in *Astutuli* when the impatiently waiting and heavily cheated *Burger* [citizens] try to control their anxiety in a naïve-absurd reflection about waiting: "time needs its time – time needs its time."

In addition to *Astutuli*, time plays an important role in several other of Carl Orff's stage works. Two further examples are:

- The Wheel of Fortune is well-known as a central theme in *Carmina Burana*. In its restless move it represents the recurrence of good and bad times: *O Fortuna, velut Luna statu variabilis...* (O Fortune, like the moon you are changeable...)
- Time has central importance in Orff's final stage work, *De temporum fine comoedia* (Play of the End of Time).

This interaction of "time remote and timelessness" can be applied to Carl Orff's complete artistic and perhaps personal awareness of time. It refers to what was stated in Chapter 3, that each of his works is based on a remote story. It may be a tale, it may arise from story-telling traditions or Greek mythology, or it may be a story that actually took place as in *Die Bernauerin* (which incorporates a bit of Bavarian history). Orff feels at home in history, but he is not historicizing. He discovers and lays bare themes that are in his opinion still valid in our time. Thus, the past is reborn as something that is timeless and new. It is worth in this context to look again at Orff's reaction after seeing for the first time the score of Monterverdi's *Orfeo*. He says,

> It was a concordance, that was moving and opened space for something new...here were new ground plans, here still was everything burgeoning and open for every development; here was the beginning that I was looking for...Here I hoped to sense a new way to the music on the stage, a way which could help me along. I wanted to start ab ovo. (Orff (1975) quoted in Jans, 1996, p. 76)

The importance of a real lifetime fades away in this state of timelessness. What can symbolize better how volatile and fleeting political power can be than the ups and downs of *Carmina's* Wheel of Fortune. "While he was not politically involved, Orff did not escape being influenced by the events in his environment. How could anyone?...Orff was human and he may have used poor judgement—just as we all may in our own attempts to live our lives" (Stewart, 1996, p. 6).

Omnia tempus habent	To everything there is a season
et suis spatiis transeunt	And a time to every purpose
universo sub coelo :	Under the heavens: A
tempus nascendi	time to be born and
et tempus moriendi	a time to die; a
tempus plantandi	time to plant and
et tempus evellendi	a time to pluck up that
quod plantatum est	which is planted, a
tempus occidendi	time to kill and
et tempus sanandi	a time to heal; a
tempus destruendi	time to break down and
et tempus aedificandi	a time to build up; a
tempus fiendi	time to weep and
et tempus ridendi	a time to laugh; a
tempus plangendi	time to mourn and
et tempus saltandi	a time to dance; a
tempus spargendi lapides	time to cast away stones and
et tempus colligendi	a time to gather stones together; a
tempus amplexandi	time to embrace and
et tempus longe fieri	a time to refrain from
ab amplexibus	embracing; a
tempus acquirendi	time to get and
et tempus perdendi	a time to lose; a
tempus custodiendi	time to keep and
et tempus abjiciendi	a time to cast away; a
tempus scindendi	time to rend and
et tempus consuendi	a time to sew; a
tempus tacendi	time to keep silence and
et tempus loquendi	a time to speak; a
tempus dilectionis	time to love and
et tempus odii	a time to hate; a
tempus belli	time of war and
et tempus pacis!	a time of peace.

Carl Orff chose this meditation about the ambivalence of time from Ecclesiastes (3,1–8) in his composition for a six-voice male choir under the main title *Sunt Lacrimae Rerum* (which also uses text from Virgil's *Aeneid*).

CHAPTER 5
But Don't Forget Gunild!

A bright shining sun can completely shade away other stars that stay close to them but cannot reach the same luminance. It is not solely a physical law; it is also valid in the human world. Gunild Keetman is such a star who could easily be overlooked. It is possible to talk about Orff Schulwerk without ever mentioning Keetman. "Orff Schulwerk" and "Orff" are quite often used synonymously. Groups of early childhood music educators are "Orff groups," and it is quite normal to talk about the "Orff instruments" and "Orff ensembles." Even "to orff" can be a trendy expression for playing with the elemental percussion instruments. The predominance of the name of Orff as an already famous composer may give an explanation for that. But we must not forget that being a woman at that time—especially an extremely shy woman (Maschat, 2004, p. 74)—did not help her to achieve adequate recognition as a composer.

Of course, there are some attempts to rightly honor her name. AOSA, the Orff Schulwerk Association of the USA, has established the Keetman Assistance Fund to support professional development and music pedagogical projects of its members. The theater room of the Carl Orff Institute in Salzburg carries her name. But still an effort must continually be made to give her the credit she deserves.

Minna Ronnefeld,[1] a close collaborator and friend of Keetman remembers:

> Sometimes, after a piece from the Schulwerk, the announcer on the radio would say: 'You've just heard a piece by Carl Orff.' This even happened with The Christmas Story, which is known to be her composition—whereat, irritated and annoyed, Gunild looked at me, slapped her thigh and burst out with 'No! I composed that!' She often had similar experiences over the years and mostly generously ignored them. (Ronnefeld, 2004b, p. 48)

Even on the cover of the score of *Die Weihnachtsgeschichte* (The Christmas Story) for the radio recordings is printed "Carl Orff—*Die Weihnachtsgeschichte;*" what Carl Orff amended by hand: "Music–Keetman" (Ronnefeld, p. 49).

---

1 See Ronnefeld (2004) p. 178 for her "personal fragments from working on collaborative projects" with Keetman.

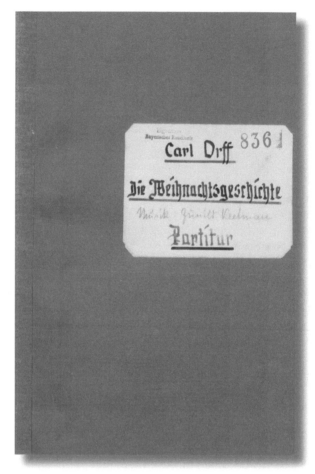

Cover of the score of *Die Weinachtsgeschichte* used for the radio production.
Carl Orff himself added handwritten "Musik Gunild Keetman."
Sammlung Liselotte Orff; Carl-Orff-Stiftung/Archiv: Orff-Zentrum München

Carl Orff the visionary, and Gunild Keetman the executing practitioner. Even if this picture serves a well-known cliché, it does not accurately represent the reality. Certainly Carl Orff, who was Keetman's teacher when she entered the Günther-Schule, had already developed and displayed the theoretical foundation of his elemental music. It was obvious that Keetman could put the Schulwerk masterly into practice as few others could. Carl Orff is known to have said to her, "No-one can do it as you do" (Ronnefeld, 2004b, p. 38). And indeed, one can notice and admirer her pleasantly open and inviting, clear and targeted teaching style when seeing her in the summary of a series of television programs presented by Bayerischer Rundfunk between 1957 and 1959 (Kallós, 2004).

It was obviously a special gift of Keetman to inspire and motivate students of every age. Among different statements by people who worked with her we find that of Verena Maschat, an internationally recognized Orff Schulwerk teacher, who was for many years the assistant to Orff Institute Director Hermann Regner. During her childhood in Munich, she had the special opportunity to belong to the children's group that presented the Orff Schulwerk in recordings of Harmonia Mundi and later (by the end of the 1950s) on television. She remembers about that time:

> We worked with models from the Schulwerk, but Gunild always encouraged us to invent our own accompaniments, texts and melodies...Gunild's way to work was purposeful and exact. It followed a secure path, and everyone practiced every part. Only then it was decided who should sing the first or the second part, who should play the bass and who the melody on the recorder...We repeated often, listened critically, kept improving until everything flowed as a matter of course. But we never had the feeling of a tiresome 'rehearsal;' somehow Gunild always knew how to keep our interest alive. (Maschat, 2004, p. 72)

Also, Verena Maschat's observations about Keetman's character would be confirmed by others who knew her well:

> I visited Gunild in her mill on a number of occasions...Always there was the committed, lovable, modest person. Conversation with her was always a dialogue, a calm alternation of listening, reflection and talking. Not wordy but to the point, with humor and spontaneity. She preferred the small group, the practical work with children and students, the learning from and with one another. The performance situation, being 'in the limelight' and having to project to others at conferences or concerts cost her a real effort of will. (p. 74)

In this context it is not surprising that her theoretical and practical reflection, *Elementaria—First Acquaintance with Orff-Schulwerk* (1974/1970), appeared more than 20 years after the start of the Schulwerk radio programs. It is "the best there is for a real acquaintance with Schulwerk..." says Werner Thomas (2004/1991, p. 156), remembering that it literally "was wrung out of her by Orff. To overcome the birth pains of a book, one moment tears flowed, the next she jestingly called her mentor 'slave-driver,' 'slave-owner.'" But "it has contributed to the fact that her name has gone round the world together with Orff's." Indeed 50 years later her book is still relevant, following the description of Martha M. O'Hehir (2020, p. 59) who writes that *Elementaria* is "... a key to unlocking and understanding the secrets and magic of what the Orff Schulwerk philosophy and practice is, how to facilitate it, and how to sequence it, for any class, community, age group."

By 1948, when the plans for the radio program were being put into practice, Gunild Keetman had advanced to the status of co-author, composer, and collaborator. It seems likely that the Schulwerk never would have been realized without her consequential and dedicated cooperation. Therefore, the title *Orff-Schulwerk—Musik für Kinder* incorporates Orff and Keetman as equivalent originators, i.e., the author's rights for the *Orff-Schulwerk—Musik für Kinder* pieces belong equally to both of them. Additionally, Gunild Keetman's cooperation with Orff was not limited to the Schulwerk:

> Through all the years Orff often asked her to come to him in Diessen, mainly to try out various questions of timbre in his compositions. Thus, she continually found herself involved in the creative process of his works, and was, as only a few know, much more than the co-author of the Schulwerk. (Ronnefeld, 2004b, p. 42)

It was Keetman who was decisive in building the bridge that connected the Schulwerk radio programs to a well-established system of foundational and further professional training. Even though the radio programs had awakened interest and even excitement among the teachers, many did not understand how to implement the Schulwerk ideas as they were intended.

There was misunderstanding from the beginning, and some teachers fell back into traditional teaching practices that excluded creativity on the part of the students. In addition, dance and movement were underrepresented in a radio program that was necessarily limited to verbal invitations and suggestions. It became more and more evident that the radio programs may have served as a very effective starting point in order to get the attention of the teachers, but they were not enough to bring Orff and Keetman's concept of elemental music education in its entirety to the classroom. Further training was necessary.

Help came from Eberhard Preussner, a man who Orff had known since 1930 when he had established the connection between Carl Orff and Leo Kestenberg in the Ministry of Culture in Berlin. Now Preussner was a professor (and later director) at the Academy of Music and Performing Arts in Salzburg, Austria (today, the Mozarteum, University for Music and Performing Arts). Beginning during the summer of 1949, he hosted music classes for children at the Mozarteum, with Gunild Keetman as the teacher. This program of music education in practice was the starting point of an evolution that made it possible for Orff Schulwerk to outlast the transmission time on the radio. It was the first impulse that led in 1963 to the inauguration of the Carl Orff-Institute, as a special department of the Mozarteum.

Keetman's indispensable collaboration in the successful Orff Schulwerk project should not let us ignore her artistic competence as a composer. In her time at the Günther-Schule (she started there as a student in 1926, and directly after her final exam in 1928 she became a member of the staff), she cooperated closely with Maja Lex who was in charge of the choreographic work for the Günther-Schule Dance Ensemble. Nearly 70 dance pieces are documented as written for this ensemble by Gunild Keetman. These were performed in presentations, competitions, and on many national and international tours.

It is interesting to compare the paths taken by Keetman and Orff to their eventual collaborations. Carl Orff was born in 1895 in Munich, in the south of Germany, Gunild Keetman in 1904 in the north, in Elberfeld (today an urban district of Wuppertal). But apart from their different geographic origins they had much in common. Both came from well-off families where music, especially active music making, played an important role.

Gunild Keetman at age two.
Carl-Orff-Stiftung/Archiv: Orff-Zentrum München

Keetman's mother played guitar and piano, and her father found his artistic expression in photography (Ronnefeld, 2004b, p. 16). Both Orff and Keetman had well-protected child-hoods, and their parents expected them to follow traditional professional careers, which neither fulfilled. Similarly, like Carl Orff who failed "to survive" school and later abandoned the Academy, Keetman's professional career was full of detours and dead ends.

It appears almost comical that she obeyed her parents—as a well-educated and dutiful daughter—to enroll in the German School for Women on the Bodensee. It was not a successful move, even after a second try in a different Women's School for Home Economics. Minna Ronnefeld (2004b, p. 20) comments: "Her school reports certainly didn't give the impression that Gunild was dreaming of a future involving cooking, ironing, or even rearing poultry." She enrolled at Bonn University in subjects of History of Art and History of Music. But she recognized quite soon that theory-oriented, academic studies did not provide perspectives for her interest. She left after only one semester.

It is so similar to what we have read about Orff's experience with school and studies: "The time at the secondary school…became almost a torment, as it held me off principally from what I wanted to do and from what I believed I had to do" (Orff, 1975a, p. 39), and "the whole Academy was conservative and patriarchal" (p. 44).

But Keetman's educational journey had not yet come to an end. She went to Berlin to enroll at the College for Physical Education. This was also not the right place for her. She found the "militant atmosphere" unbearable and left after only one semester (Ronnefeld, 2004b, p. 20). It was such a long way to the Günther-Schule in Munich. She arrived full of negative impressions about schools and self-doubts, and here she met Carl Orff. Two explorers came together in a musical world that was so different from all they had experienced before.

Gunild Keetman was fascinated by Orff's personality and charisma:

> The genius of Orff's committed teaching stood in complete contrast to everything I had previously experienced. When he sat down at the piano and started to play…he charmed forth new qualities of sound, and managed to impress upon us unforgettably, by means of examples that came to him on the spur of the moment, all the various musical styles. Or he would improvise with new and surprising sounds and could hardly bring it to an end…Not one of us students would ever have had the idea of playing something of our own…Now for hours we hardly ever came away from the piano. (Keetman, 2011/1978, pp. 50–52)

Later Keetman commented to Mina Ronnefeld (2013/2002, p. 82):

> I, and also my fellow students of whom many were just 17-18 years old, had at first only one thing in mind: the unfolding and development of our personalities through Music and Dance. We were not interested in theories; pedagogy was a foreign word; no one thought in the remotest way about teaching children.

Ronnefeld (p. 97) continues:

> Orff soon recognized Keetman's slumbering creative potential. This released a radical change in her feelings about life and freed a powerful energy for work. The work became her life and the school her home, her world. She was soon to undertake a supporting role in the further development of the Günther School.

The "predominant role" is what she also personified at the "second birth" of the Orff Schulwerk in the 1948 radio programs. It is her immeasurable contribution that makes Orff Schulwerk what it is today all over the world.

We have to look closely, but in fact there are TWO bright stars in the Orff Schulwerk sky.

CHAPTER 6
Orff Schulwerk—And What Is That?[1]

As popular as the Orff Schulwerk may be all over the world, it is not easy to find a precise definition of what it is. The name "Orff Schulwerk" does not help as an explanation. It even may lead to a misunderstanding. It can be said that it has nothing to do with traditional "school-work" like math sheets and so on. Surely it is influenced by the philosophy of Georg Kerschensteiner (1854–1932) and his idea of organizing "activity schools." Kerschensteiner included in this type of primary school (*Arbeitsschule*) workshops, kitchens, laboratories, and gardens (at that time the Bavarian version of learning by doing). According to Michael Kugler (Widmer, 2011, p. 21), the first part of the name *Schul*—does not refer to *Schule* (school) but has to be understood as the verb *schulen*—to instruct, to train, and to practice. So, Orff Schulwerk does not mean more than "the music pedagogical concept of Carl Orff" and does not solve our problem. Schulwerk was a newly coined word in the early 20th century that can also be found in Paul Hindemith's works (*Schulwerk für Instrumentalspiel*, op. 44, 1927) and as the title of violin manuals (*Geigen-Schulwerk*, 1932–1950) by Erich and Elma Doflein. At the very least, a comparison of these three "*Schulwerks*" shows a fundamental similarity. Rather than using simple exercises, all three concepts employ authentic compositions that correspond to the learner's ability.

So, what is "Orff Schulwerk" actually? Does the term Orff Schulwerk represent only the printed material in the five volumes of *Musik für Kinder* (Orff & Keetman, 1950–1954)? Does it stand for a particular teaching style in music pedagogy, or in general for unconventional, creative activities with children in the area of music, dance, and speech? With such fundamental questions, it is not surprising that there have always been attempts to define its essential characteristics in an understandable way.

We can assume that even Carl Orff himself was aware that the description of the essentials of his Schulwerk resisted a simple straightforward definition. Thus, he starts his oft-quoted 1963 lecture "Das Orff-Schulwerk–Rückblick und Ausblick" (Orff-Schulwerk–Past & Future) (Orff, 2011b/1964) with this fundamental question (Note that many years after his pedagogical ideas had already found their international recognition, he still approached his work as a question). His answer helps only indirectly and leaves room for individual interpretation. He points to the history of its origin, referring to the prehistory in the Günther-Schule and the practical implementation after the school radio programs. In this context, he also uses his much-cited picture of the *Wildwuchs*—in English, rank growth. Margaret Murray translated this as "wildflower," and that has become a beloved image for Orff Schulwerk practitioners worldwide. However, the word *Wildwuchs* also includes weeds and everything that grows near fences and paths, which gives it a slightly different meaning. In either case, we learn that the

---

1 Some of the material in this chapter has appeared elsewhere. Initially on the website of the International Orff-Schulwerk Forum Salzburg, portions have been translated and printed in publications and/or websites of Orff Schulwerk associations in Spain, Argentina, Colombia, Russia, Turkey, Greece, and the United States.

Schulwerk is NOT the result of a clearly thought-out didactic plan and that it can exist and be effective even without systematization.

With this in mind, it would be natural to call Schulwerk exclusively the published material in the well-known five volumes by Orff and Keetman and the supplementary editions. But in actual practice, recognized experts in Orff Schulwerk teaching in an international summer course may use only some of this source material, and quite often they lean more towards songs and dances from a variety of cultures, as well as creating structures for improvisation and composition using the collective creativity of the group. Given that reality, the above definition would be too narrow.

The musical reality of our time has changed considerably, and most teachers recognize that it cannot now be represented exclusively by the musical language of Orff and Keetman. The artistic and aesthetic quality of Orff and Keetman's compositions is beyond any doubt, but the compositions alone do not cover the full territory of this work. It is also important to note that a printed representation of dance and movement in general is very difficult. Therefore, in the volumes mentioned, dance, as one of the fundamental aspects of Orff Schulwerk, is limited to a few notes in the appendix. To summarize all these considerations, we must recognize once again that the term Orff Schulwerk evades a simple definition and that it may lose itself in vagueness and can lead to misinterpretations.

In order to find a valid definition of Orff Schulwerk, we have to put the teaching process into the center. It has to be defined by the characteristics that should be present in the classroom to realize Orff's main objective—the active and creative participation of the students. We call these features the "Principles of Orff Schulwerk" (Hartmann, 2019, p. 8). Of course, some of these principles may also apply to other music educational concepts. But we only speak of a working and teaching style that corresponds to the Orff Schulwerk if all these characteristics are present and are incorporated into the process.

1. The individual (the child, the student) is at the center.

Undoubtedly other music pedagogical concepts will also claim this principle. Therefore, a more detailed explanation must be given. Carl Orff's intention is that the students experience themselves as creative persons and thereby grow in personal qualities. Orff (2011b/1964, p. 154) calls it *Menschenbildung*—the development of human character. The objective of the Orff Schulwerk is not primarily to learn music and music theory in order to find one's own musical expression. It is rather that students can create their own music in order to understand music. The short music pieces, dances, and songs in the five volumes are intended to inspire, to be models and examples for work in the classroom. Of course, the teacher helps in the development process so that the students can identify with it as their music. One can describe it with the following picture: Orff Schulwerk does not want to lead the child to ("great") music, but instead, to bring music to the child. When children experience themselves as music-makers in the way described, one can expect that they are motivated to search for the great world of music in its fascinating variety over time. The concept of Orff and Keetman is learning music by making music, in contrast to the traditional way of learning in order to be able to make music.

2. The social dimension is central to the work.

Group work is the social form of teaching best suited to the Orff Schulwerk. Everyone learns from everyone; rivalries and tendencies to compete are to be avoided carefully. This requires corresponding conduct from the teacher, for the teacher should not be the prominent, all-important figure. Instead, the teacher points the way and makes suggestions, while giving the students enough room to co-determine and promote forms of cooperation. In the group, the various forms of expression in their interactions (dancing, singing, and speaking) can be experienced with one's fellow musicians.

3. Music is an integral term.

"Elemental music is never music alone but forms a unity with movement, dance, and speech. It is music that one makes oneself, in which one takes part not as a listener but as a participant" (Orff, 2011b/1964, p. 144). Therefore, when we speak about elemental music in the Orff Schulwerk, it is always understood that singing, dancing, playing instruments are equal, complementary, and connected forms of expression. Carl Orff drew from important impulses in scientific literature, especially from Curt Sachs (*Vergleichende Musikwissenschaft*, Heidelberg 1930/1959) and Fritz Brehmer (*Melodieauffassung und melodische Begabung des Kindes*, Leipzig 1925/1959) (Kugler, 2011, p. 24–26). Later, he found this interplay and unity of the different artistic activities realized in the ancient Greek theater where all forms of representation were summarized, from singing to declamation, dancing, and instrumental playing, under the term *musike techne*. This wide-ranging musical concept of the Orff Schulwerk also invites stretching the arch further and creating bridges to other artistic forms of expression—for example, to the visual arts or poetry.[1]

Dorothee Günther (2011/1932) writes on this topic:

> A person sensitive to movement...can also experience movement visually; if we give them a piece of clay...they will be able with very little practice to create sculptures that are movement-related and spontaneous. It will be the same if we give them a pencil; the movement pictures that are drawn will relatively quickly acquire life...Above all—a sense of one's own security awakens an interest in unfamiliar forms, one sees, hears, feels in other areas and there grows a sincere interest for artistic creation that has not been imposed externally. (pp. 88–90)

4. Creativity in improvisation and composition is at the start, middle, and finish.

In our perception of Western music, creativity is usually only acknowledged in outstanding persons—composers as music creators and musicians who improvise in a masterful way. Thus, creativity in the musical development of a person is admitted very late, as the perfection of a musician. The overwhelming majority of active musicians (apart from the area of jazz and some folk music) are consequently only in the area of reproducing. In dance, there is a similar development: Improvisational collaboration became a recognized way of working in choreography only in the second half of the 20th century.

Orff wanted to go the opposite way: Music making should *emerge* from improvising. The students should be able to experience creative activity from the beginning, be it in their own improvisation with three notes on a xylophone, in finding a sequence of steps to a given melody, in a movement improvisation, or in a personal arrangement of a text. (These ideas are developed further in the two articles at the end of this book.)

---

1   In a conversation with Barbara Haselbach on February 8, 2017.

Carl Orff and Gunild Keetman experimenting on the open piano (1979).
Copyright © Hannelore Gassner

5. Process and product work hand in hand to develop an artistic result.

If we compare professional activities of musicians and dancers with the work in music education, we find a major difference. In the professional field, it is usually only about the preparation for the best possible performance and the rehearsal phase is kept as short and efficient as possible. This is possible because the acting musicians and dancers have professional training, and it is necessary for economic reasons.

A music teacher who thinks and works in the same way—just focusing on the final performance—makes a serious mistake. In the classroom, the developmental process is highly important. It is the phase in which learning happens. It needs time and there should always be enough space for the students to contribute their own ideas. To come as fast as possible to the final result would not allow for trying out different solutions in order to gain personal experience. This requires notable methodical skill on the part of the teacher. Surely Orff Schulwerk cannot be called a method because there is no specified didactic procedure or obligatory methodical system to follow. However, teaching without thinking in methodical structures is not possible. Each teacher is responsible for practical implementation of lessons in the classroom and therefore has to find the appropriate methodical steps.

We talk about process-oriented teaching in Orff Schulwerk. This means that the goal is open enough to include the students' suggestions and creative contributions in the result. A lesson, such as learning a fixed instrumental piece in several parts or a dance form prepared by the teacher, can only be called an Orff Schulwerk lesson if this instructor-led unit is preceded or followed by sessions with relevant creative phases. Teaching that does not aim to engage and further the creative potential of the students can hardly be called Orff Schulwerk. (More about the meaning of "process" in Orff Schulwerk can be found in Chapter 8.)

Of course, such a teaching process only makes sense if the final result is presented to others, be it in the classroom to the classmates or in a performance for the parents. This intention of a final version is an important aspect in the creative process. After searching, finding, and testing of different options it is necessary to make decisions in order to select the final version. The educational path (process) and the artistic results (product) and their interactions—corresponding to the level and ability of the students—cannot be separated from each other in Orff Schulwerk.

6. The Orff ensemble offers a unique child-sized orchestra.

It was a main objective of Carl Orff that children could express themselves through instrumental activities as well as singing and dancing. Normally, musical instruments are connected with a long, technically oriented process of studying to reach the level of being able to play the instrument. Carl Orff had a different idea. For him, instrument playing also includes sound gestures like clapping, snapping, knee slapping, and stamping along with using any material that produces sound. But in the center are small, easy-to-use percussion instruments, including the barred instruments (xylophone, metallophone, and glockenspiel). The use of these instruments unlocked a completely new approach for music pedagogy. Consequently, the xylophone became the visual trademark of Orff Schulwerk. Unfortunately, some believe that the mere use of the percussion instruments put together by Carl Orff is sufficient to characterize an Orff Schulwerk music education activity. Carl Orff was aware of this danger. In 1963 he complained that "mistaken interpretations and the nonsensical use of the instruments threatened in many places to turn the whole meaning of the Schulwerk into the very opposite of what had been intended" (Orff, 2011b/1964, p. 150).

This "elemental instrumentarium" offers simple technique wedded to quality sound accessible to all without tedious practice. Thus, a creative approach is possible from the beginning and it is not necessary to overcome technical hurdles in order to experience the joy of instrumental music making. Additionally, the use of these movement-orientated instruments represents an ideal connection to movement and dance (Orff, 2011a/1932, p. 100).

7. Orff Schulwerk can be used in all areas of music and dance education.

At the second birth of the Orff Schulwerk as an educational radio program in 1948, the target group was precisely defined: The Orff Schulwerk should find its way into the primary school in Orff's homeland of Bavaria. Today, the aim is no longer exclusively the primary school. The Schulwerk is firmly established in early childhood music and movement education, with extensions into middle school, as well as therapeutic work, inclusive pedagogy, and activities for seniors.

Of course, each of these areas requires an adequate selection of material and activities. The music presented in volumes four and five of *Music for Children*, as well as the numerous supplements such as *Paralipomena* show clearly that working in the style of the Schulwerk can continue during the secondary level. Orff's volumes for piano and violin show the way to the application in instrumental teaching (Orff, 1934a & 1934b). (See Chapter 10 about Orff Schulwerk and instrumental learning.)

8. As an educational practice, Orff Schulwerk can also be implemented in other cultures.

Orff and Keetman's pedagogical concept was not limited to Bavaria in Germany. The international dissemination began shortly after the first radio transmissions of the Schulwerk. Music pedagogues from other countries such as Canada, Japan, Great Britain, and Argentina realized that Orff and Keetman's ideas could also be applied in their countries. Today, Orff Schulwerk can be found all over the world, with Orff Schulwerk associations in more than 40 countries. However, a prerequisite is that songs, dances, and texts have to be taken from the respective cultural area. Orff himself pointed out these necessary modifications.

> *When you work with the Schulwerk abroad, you must start all over again from the experience of the local children. And the experiences of children in Africa are different*

from those in Hamburg or Stralsund, and again from those in Paris or Tokyo. (Regner, 2011/1984, p. 220)

In summary, an authentic Orff Schulwerk experience can be defined by certain characteristics in which ALL have to be present in the way of teaching. Orff Schulwerk is not a firmly formed system—it recognizes and welcomes change. However, any extensions, modifications, and additions must be made in a careful and conscious way. This requires knowledge and deep understanding of Carl Orff's educational work. Only in this way can the fundamental principles presented here be preserved in their entirety. Orff transferred the responsibility for further work to all those who want to include Orff Schulwerk in their teaching. Thus, we understand the final words of his speech "Orff-Schulwerk - Past and Future," when Orff concludes with the first line of a quote by Schiller: "I have done my part..." (Orff, 2011b/1964, p. 156).[1]

---

1   "...Now do yours." (Thus ends Schiller's play *Don Carlos*)

CHAPTER 7
"Always Growing…"—The Music of the Schulwerk

The echo to the Schulwerk radio programs was from the start surprisingly strong, but the broadcasts passed by quite quickly and recording devices for the teachers did not yet exist. Therefore, the teachers who followed the programs on the radio with their students were missing printed music. In 1950, a request came from the Schott Publishing House asking Orff and Keetman to publish all the scores that were used in the radio programs.

However, teachers expecting methodical or even didactic hints from the books were disappointed. Orff and Keetman did not see any necessity for further explanation because they understood the printed material simply as supplemental to the radio broadcasts. While there was no connection to the sequence in which the music appeared in the radio programs, Orff and Keetman revised the large number of loose manuscripts and subdivided them according to simple musicological criteria in the following five books:

Volume I: music in Pentatonic
Volume II: music in Major limited to accompaniment by Drone Bass (Bordun) and Triads
Volume III: music in Major using Dominant and Subdominant Triads
Volume IV: music in Minor and Modes with Drone Bass (Bordun) and Triads
Volume V: music in Minor using Dominant and Subdominant Triads

That fact that the pieces offered in Volume I are simpler than those in the later ones is because Orff and Keetman followed basic logical thinking to begin with something easy to handle. It must not be understood as an elaborate teaching concept from the simple to the complicated.

The first piece in Volume I,[1] "Cuckoo, where are you?" uses only g and e. The descending minor third, sol – mi, seems to be the same starting point used in the Kodály concept. But this apparent similarity shows exactly the difference: While in the Kodály concept the interval of a minor third represents the starting point of a well-thought-out system that uses clearly defined methodical steps, no systematization is intended in the Schulwerk. There is no sequence to follow, and it is no wonder that the next pieces are of a different technical and musical level.[2]

This loosely structured collection of pieces, songs, and dances presented under the title *Orff-Schulwerk—Music for Children* may sometimes create an understandable uneasiness for teachers. Everyone who works in a school system has to follow a didactic concept. But in reference to Orff Schulwerk this has to be done by every teacher individually according to the official curriculum of their school. To project this professional duty into an intention of Orff and Keetman is just wrong. Orff was never interested in imposing this, and he makes it clear in this statement: "Most methodical, dogmatic people derive scant pleasure from [the Schul-

---

1   Unless otherwise stated, examples in this chapter refer to pages in the English adaptation of *Orff-Schulwerk Music for Children* Volumes 1–5 by Margaret Murray (1958–1966), Schott Music.
2   If Orff and Keetman really had a didactic concept in mind, some complex pieces like Nr. 38 on page 123 in Volume I would not be understandable.

werk], but those who are artistic and who are improvisers by temperament enjoy it all the more" (Orff, 2011b/1964, p. 134). It can present a challenge for teachers. A similar misunderstanding occurs with pieces that were designed as models for students' improvisations. Very often they are treated as little compositions, which Michael Kugler tells us is, "a basic, virtually classic misinterpretation, which persecutes the Orff-Schulwerk till today" (Kugler, 2000, p. 243). In 1954 Schott published Wilhelm Keller's *Einführung in Musik für Kinder—Orff-Schulwerk* (Introduction to *Music for Children*), which helped a little to explain how to use Orff and Keetman's ideas. But obviously following Orff's concept of "no didactic!" the information is kept very general.

We have to accept that *Music for Children* is not a textbook or a manual that gives methodical help about how to teach a certain piece, a dance, or a song. This lack of didactic structure is mentioned by Carl Orff again and again:

> *Schulwerk has grown from ideas that were rife at that time and that found their favorable conditions in my work. Schulwerk did not develop from any pre-considered plan—I could never have imagined such a far-reaching one—but it came from a need that I was able to recognize as such.* (Orff, 2011b/1964, p. 134)

And in the foreword to the last of the five Orff Schulwerk volumes he accentuates the incompleteness of his Schulwerk again:

> *The five volumes contain the experiences from nearly thirty years' work. Nevertheless, this first attempt to lay the foundations in print can only include a fragment of the inherent possibilities. To avoid the danger of diffusion, and in order not to disturb the structural unity of the work as a whole, many ideas have been barely suggested, and countless sources of material have had to be omitted. May this be a stimulant and starting point for those teachers that follow. It has been written for the young and to them it is dedicated.* (Orff & Keetman, Vol. V, 1966, no page)

"Every phase of Schulwerk will always provide stimulation for new independent growth; therefore, it is never conclusive and settled…always growing, always flowing" (Orff, 2011b/1964, p. 134). With these sincere and even humble words, Carl Orff pointed out that he saw himself only as the starting impulse. He invites teachers to enrich and even modify the basic materials in order to adapt them to the particular age of the students, to the specific cultural area, and to the progression of time. But he adds immediately a profound concern: "Herein of course lies a great danger, that of development in the wrong direction. Further independent growth presupposes basic specialist training and absolute familiarity with the style, the possibilities, and the aims of Schulwerk" (p. 134). In order to find out what new musical materials could be appropriately used in the sense of the Schulwerk we have to look first to the original material that Orff and Keetman published in the five volumes of *Musik für Kinder* (Orff & Keetman, 1950–1954), and respectively in the English adaptation by Margaret Murray, *Music for Children* (1958–1966).

Carl Orff and Gunild Keetman working on a score (1981).
© Hannelore Gassner

The musical material Orff and Keetman used included rhymes, songs, riddles, count-ing-out rhymes. We can assume there are many pieces that Carl Orff connected with his own childhood—Bavarian dialect included. Carl Orff's friend and adviser, Werner Thomas, in an interview that he gave to me for my radio programs, called it *Altgold* (old gold)—folk poetry and songs that already had their value in the past.

The rhythmic and melodic exercises are worthy of note. They appear only in the first and the last volumes, but their importance is emphasized in the forewords of the volumes between:

- In Volumes II and III: "For 'Rhythmic Exercises' those in volume one should be continued" (1959, no page number; 1963, no page number).
- In Volume IV we read: "The rhythmic exercises in volume five should be practiced concur-rently with this volume" (1966, no page number).

Also noteworthy is how the activities are listed in a straightforward, almost uninspiring way. As an example, on page 82 of Volume I there are "Ostinato exercises for tuned percussion instruments" with 95(!) variations of the drone bass C/G. Teachers who think they have to work through all these options would become desperate. Orff and Keetman wanted only to show what variations are possible. They left for the teachers the task of inspiring their students to find some of this variety in a creative teaching manner.

Some rhymes and songs in the original volumes may startle us with their subject matter. Volume IV of the German edition begins with: *Bet' Kinder bet', morgen kommt der Schwed*[1] (Orff & Keetman, 1954, p. 1), which is a children's song from the time of the Thirty Years' War. There are also some unusual rhymes in Volume I (German edition), for example, this Bavarian children's verse to be used as a speech exercise: *Rumpedibum, der Kaiser schlagt um, mit Händ und mit Füss, mit feurigem Spiess, hat d'Fenster eingschlagen, hat's Blei davontragn, hat Kugeln draus gossn und d'Bauern erschossen*[2] (Orff & Keetman, 1950, p. 27).

Even though these questionable choices are few, there arises the question of how appropriate they are for school. We know, in 1948 with the start of the Schulwerk radio programs, the war

---

1 "Pray children, pray, tomorrow comes the Swede."
2 "Rumpedibum, the Emperor lashes about, with hands and with feet, with a fiery spear, has battered the windows, has taken away the lead, has cast bullets from it and shot the farmers dead."

was just over and still a reality in the memories of the children. On the other hand, nowadays seeing acts of war on television news and in movies almost daily, playing war on the playground or with video games, why not broach the horror and dark face of war in a historical and artful view, in an appropriate way respecting the age of the students? Carl Orff found these texts in *Des Knaben Wunderhorn: Alte deutsche Lieder* (The Boy's Magic Horn: Old German Songs). It was a popular and recognized collection of old folk rhymes and songs, edited by the poets Achim von Arnim and Clemens von Brentano, first published in 1805. Whatever Orff was thinking about its pedagogical appropriateness, it shows his previously mentioned strong connection to history. And again, Orff was an artist and art also has the right to provoke.

Looking at *Johann, spann an* in the German edition Volume V (Orff & Keetman, 1954, p. 16), we effectively see the witches with their cat-drawn buggy hurrying up the Blocksberg mountain to their annual meeting. Some pages later we find a musical version of the *Hexeneinmaleins* (Witches' multiplication table) (p. 124; Murray ed., p. 113) from Goethe's *Faust*:

Du mußt verstehn! Aus Eins mach Zehn	Now don't delay! From one make ten
Und Zwei laß gehn,	take two away,
und Drei mach gleich, so bist du reich.	add three again, the four affix.
Verlier die Vier! Aus Fünf und Sechs,	If you'd be rich, from five and six,
so sagt die Hex,	so says the witch,
mach Sieben und Acht, so ist's vollbracht:	make seven and eight, and seal your fate,
Und Neun ist Eins, und Zehn ist Keins.	and nine is one, and ten is none.
Das ist das Hexen-Einmaleins.	Done is the witches' one times one.

It is art. It's authentic. If you go through the Orff Schulwerk volumes you will find nothing that is sweet, cute, and nicely made up for children. We have to think about that when we add our own songs and pieces to the Schulwerk. It is common sense that there is no accounting for taste, but we should feel a clear responsibility if we add new content to the Schulwerk. As Orff made clear, the Schulwerk should never feel content and settled, but it must grow and flow forward on the basis of its primary artistic aesthetic. That is what keeps it honest and true.

CHAPTER 8
Teaching Orff—Teaching Creativity

It is always intriguing to talk with students about what makes a good teacher. The answers are quite similar whether they are school-age children or young adults training to become teachers. You can often hear phrases like "they should understand how the students feel" "...should be patient," or "...should not show who they do or do not like," "...should not be moody." Subject-oriented professional competences appear in these discussions very often only secondary. It demonstrates how important it is that teachers are able to connect well with their students; that they take into account to whom they are speaking, respond to students' interests, and react in a human way to their weaknesses. This is the basis and precondition for learning that is free from unnecessary stress. Surely there are "born teachers"—individuals who are more advantaged by their personality (character and education) than others. We can state: "Good for the teacher and good for the students, if the teacher does everything right just by intuition, just by nature." But much more important is the fact that good teaching—including teaching a subject where the creativity of the students is a central issue—can be learned. This needs good preparation, sensitivity, and the capacity for self-reflection. In addition, listening to students and talking with colleagues can help one to grow into being a more responsive and empathetic teacher.

In an ideal situation there are two elements that should come together:

- Sound professional knowledge with corresponding musical skills.
- The capacity to transmit knowledge and skills to the students.

We call this capability Teaching Competence. In any pedagogical system, this competence on the part of the teacher should be as high as possible. In the case of students who are beginners or those who have learning difficulties, however, the teacher's ability to connect is an essential requirement.

From the student's side, there is a corresponding and complementary characteristic, a Learning Competence. In the early stages of learning something new, young children and beginners in general have a low learning competence because they have not yet gained a necessary quantity of knowledge to catalogue the incoming information in a serviceable form. Thus, a beginner on an instrument needs clear and inspiring explanations and a good amount of patience, while an advanced student already knows what is important. A lesson in a master class in a conservatory is often an exchange between a very experienced teacher and a younger learner who knows where to look and what to copy and adapt. Therefore, it can be said: The lower the learning competence the higher the teaching competence should be (see the graphic). If the learning competence is high the teaching competence is not so essential. (We know this from school: Good students have better chances of 'surviving' a poor teacher.)

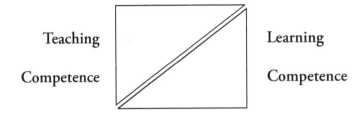

Teaching   Learning

Competence   Competence

Let us take the teacher's musical knowledge and skills as given and focus on the process of transmitting knowledge and skills to the students. While the students will benefit from a well-planned lesson, they will not be aware of how much thinking, deciding, and structuring behind the scenes the teacher must carry out in order to create a lesson that appears to the student to be so playful and easy going. Paul Brunnhuber (1971), a German pedagogue who focuses on teaching issues, has expounded on the key characteristics of successful instruction in his "Principles of Effective Lesson Planning."

a. Goal orientation
b. Motivation
c. Structuring
d. Change of activities
e. Appropriateness
f. Control and Monitoring

(These principles can also serve as a checklist to use for the purpose of evaluating successful and unsuccessful moments after completing the teaching process.)

a) Goal orientation
Every teaching activity is justified only if there is an intention to reach a certain goal or a combination of goals. For the music teacher, the goal might be singing in tune, creating movement sequences to a given melody, creating music to express an image or tell a story. To pursue a goal does not necessarily mean to have a perfect outcome at the end of a lesson. A too-detailed intended result can hinder the creative process, especially when the teacher is aiming at a prepared solution. The teacher should be aware that there can be many different types of objectives in the same lesson, e.g., intellectual, emotional, social, motor, rhythmic. Any progress toward a goal should be seen as success.

b) Motivation
It is in the nature of an Orff Schulwerk lesson to find the students motivated to participate. A playful approach is always helpful. Some teachers think that competition increases the motivation. However, this is a dangerous device, as it often leads away from the work and instead it focuses on the person—the "winner." This is not only questionable, but it also creates a ranking within the group. When an order (Who is the best?) is established after several challenges, a healthy motivation is lost.

Competition and creativity have a very problematic relationship. Contests are only justified in the professional world and should be avoided in the sphere of pedagogy.

c) Structuring

Lesson planning should reflect the right timing within the lesson. It is not only the question of what will be taught in the session, but also how and how much. Whether the teaching will be successful or not depends also on the right moment when each new piece of information is presented and in what order. It would be counter-productive to start with the most important and most complex theme at the beginning, at a moment when everyone is not yet mentally entirely present. It would likewise not make sense to put it at the end of the session, when concentration and attention are diminishing. Therefore, it is helpful that the lesson has a basic structure:

- opening activity (a warm up, a song, a rhythm game, etc.)
- main section (working on a dance, a song, an instrumental piece, a graphic notation, etc.)
- closing activity (a song, review of a previous activity, preview of further topics, etc.)

An ideal lesson plan begins with an opening activity that leads to the main theme of the day. The closing activity carries the presentation to the final result.

d) Change of activities

With its wide variety of media, an Orff Schulwerk lesson offers many different and fun activities that can be used to work on a single idea or skill. Singing, dancing, and instrument playing are the three important pillars of the Schulwerk. But it would not be realistic to use them equally in every lesson. Aiming for a rich and inspiring blend of activities should be the intention of the teacher. Such variability attracts the students' attention and allows them many different ways to understand and practice the given goal.

What a rich variety of activities an Orff Schulwerk lesson can offer!

- dancing
- instrument playing
- listening to music
- improvising and composing music, choreographing dance
- talking and discussing
- writing and painting notation

e) Appropriateness

There is a multitude of actions and decisions during a lesson that have to pass the control of being suitable and adequate. Was the piece too difficult? Was my response to the answer by a student in a certain situation appropriate? Every lesson is full of points for reflection. One decision can be right but another one may influence negatively the outcome of the lesson.

Some considerations…

a. …with reference to music:
   right pitch, correct rhythm, musically correct information.
b. …with reference to the students:
   the level of the difficulty of a music piece or a dance, finding the right intellectual level.
c. …with reference to the language used by the teacher:
   all parameters of the spoken language, like pace, volume, style of speech.

Appropriateness has to be ensured in all areas in order to achieve good teaching results. For instance, a song accompaniment that is sophisticated and musically attractive may have to be declined if it is too difficult for the students. Or a setting may be easy to play but not correct musically, e.g., remaining on a drone bass where a chord change is needed is not appropriate.

f) Control and monitoring

It is required that the teacher knows in every moment what is going on in the group. Do the students understand what they are expected to do? Are there students who have difficulties? Are there students who are distracted or are distracting others? Does every student have the correct mallets? Are the students sitting in a place where they can see the teacher? And there are a hundred things more.

Sometimes it can be very stressful to observe all of this while going on with the subject matter. The task of the teacher can be put into a picture: Teachers have to be like a lighthouse and a spotlight at the same time. They should have the overview at every moment, and simultaneously they should see where their special attention is required.

The teaching principles serve as wrap-up after a lesson

As mentioned before, this list of principles for lesson planning can also be very helpful for the self-reflection phase. Then every item can be put into one or more questions:

a) Goal orientation
- What have the students learned in the lesson?
- In what aspect have they gained competence?
- Have there been students who did not understand what we were working on?

b) Motivation
- Did the students show interest in the activities?
- What did the teacher do to make the lesson interesting to the students?
- Did the interest last through the entire lesson?

c) Structuring
- Were the students smoothly led to the main subject of the lesson?
- Was there a balanced end to the lesson?
- Was it necessary to hurry up and omit something that should have been said before leaving?

d) Change of activities
- What different activities engaged the children during the lesson?

e) Appropriateness
- Was the teaching material suitable for the age, development, and capacity of the students?
- Were modifications to the original preparation justified by the course of the lesson?
- Were the reactions of the teacher appropriate to the conduct of the students?
- Was the speaking of the teacher appropriate in speed, loudness, and vocabulary to the target group?

f) Control and monitoring
- Was the teacher aware of all interactions in the classroom (the constructive ones and the informal ones, and even disagreements between students)?
- Did the teacher recognize when a student had a problem?

The comments and reflections in this chapter about the teaching process and lesson planning can be applied to every teaching system and subject, from geography to mathematics. But to teach Orff Schulwerk in an appropriate way, there is more.

What makes Orff Schulwerk teaching so special is the focus on creativity. We must never forget that the main goal of Carl Orff and Gunild Keetman is to help students to make up their own music and their own dancing. In that sense, teachers must use their knowledge and competence in the subject to assist the students in the creative process. This double role of leading the children to the understanding and skills they do not yet have and helping them release the inherent musicality that they already have is the challenge of teaching according to Orff and Keetman's vision.

To be creative is something that has to be learned and therefore it has to be taught. If creativity happens in everyday life (i.e., not in school), it usually derives from a necessity. One may encounter a problem that has to be solved when normally used devices are not available. For example, if you have no letter opener you may take a knife, scissors, pencil, or something else to open a well-sealed envelope—a basic form of creativity. Imagination and divergent thinking are needed to find a solution for a pending problem, a casual difficulty, or (in school) a given assignment. In daily life what we call a problem is called a "task" in the pedagogical environment. The task has to be open enough so that different solutions can be found.

The creative process can be structured in consecutive phases:

- Define and frame the task
- Gather different possibilities for solutions
- Take the one that you (or the group) are (is) favoring and elaborate on it
- Modify and improve it and present it as the chosen solution

In this context the teacher has to handle three obligations:

a) Starting and organizing the creative process
Explain what the creative task will be. If examples are necessary, give more than one and possibly very different ones. This helps to avoid students wanting to please the teacher by imitating (to make decisions is a central obligation in a creative setting).

b) Supervising the working phase (in groups)
The teacher has to watch closely, because the rules of conduct have to be obeyed. Ensure that everyone in the group can participate actively (The "playground kings" or "queens" must not take over!). If there are opposing ideas, the teacher should mediate.

c) Evaluating the elaborated results and solutions
It has to be clear to the teacher that assessing a creative work is different from assessing any other task done by a student. If a student plays a given composition, for example, he is assessed on technical and stylistic aspects but not about the composition itself. If the student (or group) however is the creator of a piece or a dance, then he feels—and in fact is—responsible for everything.

Ulrike E. Jungmair (1992) defines the role of the teacher in elemental music and movement education as organizer and arranger, playmate and team-member. She provides, helps further, gives new suggestions. Her open teaching design and her availability make it possible for the unpredictable and un-projectable enter in the teaching and become lively reality (p. 199).

It is also important HOW the teacher expresses feedback in response to creative efforts. Here are some examples:

Avoid	Better
It is confusing.	Tell us what you wanted to do.
It's wrong, it does not work.	What can you do to improve it?
This is not a good solution.	In my opinion, this is not a good solution because…
You use only one instrument.	How would it sound if you include different instruments?
It is very short.	What can you do to make the piece a little longer?
You are good!	You created a good piece/dance.

In short, instead of personalizing the work ("you are good"), focus on the outcome and not on the person ("this is a convincing solution"). The works of different groups/students can be compared, but in a way that does not result in a ranking. ("I liked the variety of instruments this group used and this other group's change in tempo really caught my attention.")

The teacher has to be aware of how much the language used in the classroom is defining the teaching style and ultimately the working atmosphere. Self-monitoring and even recording the teaching can be very helpful. The balance of praise and critique is a central part of a healthy teacher-student relationship. Informing, explaining, proposing, advising, helps keep the process of teaching and learning in the center.

A final word on the use of the term "process" in the field of Orff Schulwerk teaching.

What is meant by "process," "Orff process," and "process teaching?" These are word combinations in use that may be understood by some, but they are still missing a clear definition. Referring to publications on the subject of pedagogy does not help either. There we find repeatedly that teaching in general is seen as a process. There is also talk about the "teaching-learning process." This identification obviously encompasses all types of teaching. So, what makes "process teaching" special? From what other teaching style should it be distinguished?

Every well-planned lesson needs a structure and consists of a sequence of meaningful methodical steps. But why should we call this flow of well-set actions in a lesson a process? Is there a reluctance to label aspects of Schulwerk teaching as methodical because the Schulwerk cannot be called a method? The pedagogy connected with Orff Schulwerk surely is not a self-contained method. Orff and Keetman clearly did not want to label any teaching procedure as the only correct one. However, no effective teaching situation can exist without a systematic strategy, including Orff Schulwerk. In this case, the planning is left to the individual teacher.

In order to give reasonable meaning to the term "process" we have to be more subtle. It is not enough to say that process is a teaching sequence where we just go from A to B in the most efficient way, as in having the students play a piece that the teacher has conceived or one as it is printed in the Orff Schulwerk volumes. A process needs more. It should include improvisation and every type of creativity on the part of the students. The outcome of the lesson should not be completely predictable at the beginning. In an "Orff process" (in this sense) the teacher has to be open—even to be challenged by the ideas of the students—to find musical results that include the students as creators. This way of teaching needs sufficient time to let the students think and explore their own concepts. It is a "play on the way… [that] can range from fun diversion to an exercise that contributes to a unique performance of the material in question" (Harding, 2013, p. 4).

If it is really an "Orff process," then creativity of the students must play a central role.

CHAPTER 9
Looking Over the Fence—Orff and the Others

The number of music pedagogical teaching strategies, methods, and concepts is too great to be listed here, and it would grow larger if we included specialized methods related to a particular instrument. But there are three music pedagogical approaches that are well-known, recognized, and successfully used in many countries throughout the world. They are connected with the names of Zoltán Kodály, Émile Jaques-Dalcroze, and Carl Orff: The Kodály Concept (frequently called Kodály Method), Dalcroze Eurhythmics, and Orff Schulwerk. The priority of these concepts is not to develop professional musicians, but to encourage all people in different ways to express themselves through music, to foster comprehension of and joy through music. Though all three share these common goals, their ways to achieve it are notably different.

People who encounter these pedagogies might be tempted to ask which is the "best." Naturally, this is not a question that can be honestly answered. All three are well-structured and have a deliberate philosophical base. Yet it is important to look closely at precisely how they differ from each other. If we look closer at the motives that put these concepts into motion, then we can recognize which are the strong elements of each, and which aspects were considered by the originator as less important.

It is important to acknowledge that the efficiency and educational repercussion of a pedagogical concept depends first and foremost on the teaching competence of the individual teacher. Surely there are teachers who are able to put such concepts in an almost ideal way into practice. But there are also those, who—even when doing everything right—have not understood the spirit and idea of the founders and consequently cannot pass them on to their students in an appropriate way.

Comparing the three music pedagogic approaches of Kodály, Jaques-Dalcroze, and Orff, we will put the following questions into the center:

- What do the three concepts have in common?
- In what ways do they differ?
- What aspects of music education does each emphasize?
- How can these approaches be used together in a complementary way?

What do the educational concepts of Kodály, Jaques-Dalcroze, and Orff have in common?
All three founders were not primarily music educators. They were musicians, or to be more precise, composers and conductors. Compositions of Kodály and Orff are frequently on programs in concert halls and theaters. Jaques-Dalcroze also had studied composition with famous teachers that included Anton Bruckner in Vienna as well as Léo Delibes and Gabriel Fauré in Paris. His work includes several operas, oratorios, and song cycles.

This quite similar professional development leads to a logical consequence—the high quality of the music used in the classroom was of primary importance. Music can be technically simple, but still be of high aesthetic quality. We know that Zoltán Kodály demanded that in music lessons, "the best is just about good enough." This can equally apply to the small instrumental pieces in the Orff Schulwerk in which each of these miniature models has a special feature. And the high demand that the Jaques-Dalcroze pedagogy puts on piano improvisation points in the same direction.

A further commonality is that the three founders were not alone when developing their systems. They could rely on competent collaborators. The Kodály system, which was built on roots reaching far back into history, would not be imaginable without the assistance of Jenö Ádám—also a composer—Erszébet Szöny, and others. The Orff Schulwerk would not exist without Orff's co-author Gunild Keetman and the first directors of the Orff Institute—Keller, Regner, and Haselbach. Dalcroze Eurhythmics would not have been the same without Wolf Dohrn, Nina Gorter, and a great number of students who developed his pedagogy into different directions.

How are these concepts different? What makes each unique?

This question can be answered best by analyzing what motivated these three artists to develop their pedagogical ideas. This helps us to understand better why each was emphasizing different aspects of music education and why some activities are the center of attention and others are less present.

The Zoltán Kodály Concept

As a composer and ethnomusicologist, Kodály was very attached to the extensive and rich treasure of Hungarian folk songs. At the same time, he was aware that active singing was practiced less and less in his country and that the oral tradition of folk songs was in danger of becoming lost. It was clear to him that a formal expansion of music lessons in the school curriculum was not enough. Kodály wanted a conscious singing. Students should not only develop singing skills, but also gain insight into the melodic, rhythmic, and harmonic aspects of the songs. The music should be *understood*. Kodály found the solution in *relative solmisation* in which the singer uses the diatonic structure of the melodic scale to hear and analyze internally a melody in order to sing it in tune. This system was already used in England with a high level of success by John Curwen (1816–1880). It had roots that go back to Guido d'Arezzo (ca. 990–1050) and the so-called Guidonian Hand. This was a medieval device used to orient oneself in the tonal system. It helped monks to sing Gregorian chant. It existed before Guido d'Arezzo but became well known with his form of application. He used the hexachord syllables *Ut, Re, Mi, Fa, Sol, La*, which represented the beginning syllables of each phrase in the Hymn to Saint John the Baptist (*Ut Queant Laxis*). Because each line started with a note higher than the line before, it helped the singer to understand the tonal structure of a melody. Many centuries later, Curwen included the well-known code of hand signs.

Kodály built his concept on Curwen's work and encouraged his collaborators to find a clear methodical structure, including the rhythmic dimension of music.

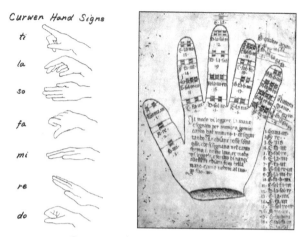

Curwen Hand Signs

ti
la
so
fa
mi
re
do

Curwen Hand Signs and Guido's Hand

We might assume that Kodaly liked to dance as much as his countrymen, and even more as an ethnomusicologist. However, dance as a possible form of musical expression is hardly mentioned in his program. This is completely understandable considering that Kodály's objective was to save the great treasure of Hungarian folksongs. Therefore, dance was not in his focus, nor did stimulating creativity have any priority in that context.

Because the learning of relative solmization depends strongly on the process of conditioning in order to connect the pitch with its name and hand sign, extensive practice is indispensable. This in turn requires a high potential of motivation by the teacher. Because the method has proven to be very effective in achieving its goals of musical literacy through singing, we may assume that the students are strongly motivated by their own progress and success.

Jaques-Dalcroze Eurythmics

Émile Jaques-Dalcroze began as a teacher of harmony and solfeggio at the Conservatory of Geneva in Switzerland. In his classes, he noticed that his students had a great deficit in rhythmic competence. This led him to develop a methodology that enabled his students to feel, experience, and learn music through their bodies. He invented exercises and playful activities to express all musical parameters through movement, from dynamics, tempo, and pitch to harmonic sequences, phrasing, and accentuation. In Dalcroze classes, the teacher controls and stimulates these exercises and movement sequences by improvising in a sensitive and tasteful way on the piano. In order to avoid confusion with dance, Jaques-Dalcroze called this movement-oriented educational concept in German *Rhythmische Gymnastik*, which became in English Dalcroze Eurhythmics, a method that is successfully applied all over the world today.

We know that for Jaques-Dalcroze, singing was also important. He composed many songs, and in the beginning of his pedagogical work he experimented with "dance songs." However, in his concept, singing lost its importance and the piano acted as a controlling element for movement.

Orff Schulwerk

We have seen here how Orff and Keetman came to realize their vision of elemental music. Its strong element is the focus on creativity within the integration of dancing, singing, and playing. As a weak point, it can be seen that Orff and Keetman rejected offering a didactic structure, which was a logical decision in their thinking. It is in the responsibility of all Orff Schulwerk teachers to adapt their instruction to the curriculum of the institution where they work. We can assume that Carl Orff and Gunild Keetman considered ear training as an important area of music education, but in the Schulwerk it does not appear as a specific goal. While Jaques-Dalcroze drew up thoroughly designed practice sequences, Orff believed that the same objectives could be accomplished in a purely playful way.

Summary of strengths and matters of less importance

Concept	Focus	Less important or lacking
Kodály Concept	Singing	Dance, improvisation, and creativity
Dalcroze Eurhythmics	Awareness and expression of all parameters of music through the body	Singing
Orff Schulwerk	Experiencing through creativity; singing, dancing, and instrument playing as a unit	Methodical guidance, ear training

In the Kodály's system, singing is at the center; Jaques-Dalcroze focuses on corporal expression; and Orff on creativity and improvisation. Who can judge which is more important or what is unnecessary?

Using the concepts in a complementary way

We know that thoughtful teachers of all three practices compensate the less considered issues by using activities from the others. Therefore, even if someone feels more closeness to one of these approaches, it is helpful to know the basic fundaments and the theoretical outlines of all. Some suggest designing a pedagogy that includes the characteristics of all the three systems. Yet by doing so, there is the danger that all three would lose bit by bit their identities and their appeal. Advice to music teachers: You may use activities from all three (and other) systems but be aware from where you take them!

It is remarkable, that all three concepts were designed with a clear purpose for a very local and therefore limited target group:

• At the beginning Zoltán Kodály was thinking exclusively about Hungarian children.
• Jaques-Dalcroze was thinking exclusively about his university students in the Conservatory of Geneva.
• Carl Orff began his work with young adult dancers in an experimental school and later designed his radio program for Bavarian primary school children whose music instruction he wanted to enrich.

In all three cases there was at the beginning no thought about any cultural export or influence in other countries. In fact, it was just the reverse—music pedagogues from other countries took notice of what was happening in Hungary, Switzerland, and Germany and became convinced that these concepts could also be applied in their homelands. Following study of these new approaches in their countries of origin, they returned to their own countries and began the work of adopting and adapting these ground-breaking ideas.

The fact that all three concepts originated in Europe may be seen critically outside of Europe. It might appear as a typical example of Eurocentrism: i.e., does the entire world always have to learn and imitate what comes from Europe? Is European thinking obligatory? It is not as simple as that. We have to take into consideration the cultural-philosophical and social development that happened in Europe. It undoubtedly constituted a certain pioneer situation worldwide. It started in the time of the Enlightenment during the 18th century with the thought and work of those geniuses who revolutionized our notions of education. In order, they are:

Jean-Jacques Rousseau
(1712–1778)

Johann Heinrich Pestalozzi
(1746–1827)

Friedrich Fröbel (Froebel)
(1782–1852)

Rudolf Steiner
(1861–1925)

Maria Montessori
(1870–1952)

These great philosophers and educators pointed out that childhood represents a special period in human life. Childhood is not simply a time of waiting to become an adult. It has its own quality and consequently includes the right to a child-oriented education. Even though this philosophy has its roots in Europe, it is surely valid for all children in the world. These fundamental ideas of the Enlightenment prepared the soil for the origin and growth of these three music pedagogies, which have importance for all human beings and consequently can be—and have been—put into practice everywhere.

Independent of these three European concepts, there also developed a science-based approach to music education in the United States. While Jaques-Dalcroze, Kodály, and Orff developed their concepts relying on their artistic intuition and pedagogic experience, an American psychologist referred to results found in test situations. Research by Carl Seashore (1967/1938) led to using tests to measure the musical ability of the population in the 20th century (the time of Günther-Schule!). Seashore's research became one of the bases for Edwin Gordon to develop his Music Learning Theory. "Music Learning Theory is an explanation of how we learn when we learn music…Music Learning Theory is a comprehensive method for teaching audiation,"[1] as it reads on the homepage of the Gordon Institute of Music Learning (Gordon Institute for Music Learning, 2021).

Gordon's great influence was putting into the center of our attention how children learn music and also in what different stages this happens. Learning music should develop the same way as we learn to speak. It starts with listening, imitating sounds, learning the logical code of a language, and at the very end of this comes writing and reading music.[2] This sounds so reasonable that we have to ask why traditional music education very often goes in the opposite direction: starting with learning the names of the notes and reading written music. These activities often occupy so much time that listening and understanding with the outer and the inner ear (a sort of audiation) never happens.

---

1 "Audiation" is Gordon's term for the ability to think music in the mind with understanding.
2 Note that the concepts of Kodály, Dalcroze, and Orff are not contradictory to this sequence.

But still there is the question of how to put Gordon's findings into practice. Because listening to music is stressed, it seems to be more important that the child is exposed to music rather than being involved in making music. Edwin Gordon as a scientist stands without question. But there are opinions that his pedagogical application "is too prescriptive and proscriptive to students and teachers" (Woodford, 1996, pp. 83–95). Gordon's ideas would be better implemented by using pedagogical concepts like those of Kodály, Orff, and others. Music should be experienced and not just administered like medicine or vitamins.

Continuing with this metaphor, we might consider Gordon to be a nutrition scientist. Then we might argue: The school needs musical "chefs" who prepare delicious "dishes" of interesting and enjoyable music lessons. Of course, all the important musical "vitamins" that nutritionists such as Gordon have discovered must be included in the "meal." Dalcroze, Orff, and Kodály are excellent master musical chefs who prepare delicious and nutritious meals, but Orff even teaches the children how to cook.

CHAPTER 10

Are We Really Playing
When We Are Playing an Instrument?
Orff Schulwerk and Its Delicate Relationship
to Instrumental Music Education

Today we find the influence of the Schulwerk in *almost* every area of music education. One encounters it working in the field of early childhood music education and, of course, in primary school, the first group addressed by the original radio programs. The process-oriented and creative way of the Schulwerk also can be applied at the secondary school level if appropriate musical materials are used. We also find Orff Schulwerk used in work with persons with special needs and in programs for seniors in residences or hospitals. The ideas and teaching activities related to the Orff Schulwerk are successfully applied in many places. So, why the restriction *almost*? It refers to the special relationship of Orff Schulwerk to the field of musical instrument teaching and learning.

Of course, there are teachers of instruments—even a few manuals for instrument teaching—that include ideas of the Orff Schulwerk approach in their instruction. However, the distance between Orff Schulwerk and instrument classes is significant. There are different opinions, even antithetic points of view. Orff suggests that children learn to handle musical instruments by doing, by experimenting. The children's first encounter with instruments should be similar to playing with toys—exploring, trying things out, *playing*. Orff mentions as examples simple instruments like "sticks, rattles, wooden boxes, etc." (Orff, 2011a/1932, p. 68), which can easily become triangle, woodblock, and hand drum in the primary school classroom.

But playing with a tringle, woodblock, and hand drum? How does this sound to a teacher of an instrument who attends to the correct technique from the very beginning? Let us think of a violin teacher who has to observe about ten parameters only regarding the right arm—the bowing arm, from shoulder to elbow, hand, and little finger, etc. Each right or wrong position and movement has direct influence on the quality of the sound (…and we have not yet mentioned the left hand, which is manipulating the pitch!). There are coordinated movements that need a long time to master, with many corrections along the way. The teacher cannot say, "Take the violin and find out what sounds it can make," as one could with a hand drum or a woodblock. Or consider a trumpet teacher, for whom breath control using the diaphragm is an indispensable condition. (A short conciliatory remark for percussionists: you can produce a rich variety of sounds on percussion instruments if you are experienced. But percussionists prove their expertise more by mastering a multitude of different instruments and by producing very complex and complicated rhythms.)

How amateur might it look to a musician when twenty children form a choir of recorders, playing together without any breath control, not thinking that the tongue should function as an articulation controller? We know, of course, that the recorder is a helpful and affordable device for learning to play from printed music. But is the recorder seen as an instrument? It is remarkable that for Carl Orff himself it was not an easy decision to include the recorder in his elemental ensemble. He regarded the recorder as an important component of Baroque music, not at all elemental. Only knowing the fact that the roots of this instrument go back to prehistoric times when this type of flute was made from animal or human bones helped Orff to change his mind. But regardless of this culturally historic issue, there remains the problem of playing the recorder technically in the right way when students are not well prepared. (A colleague in my conservatory—a recorder teacher and recognized specialist of music of Renaissance and Baroque—once said to me: "All children who started with recorder in kindergarten or primary school are lost for serious continuation with this instrument…" There may exist exceptions if they are taught by teachers who include good breath control and sensitive tonguing in their instruction. But her remark is understandable).

There are more points that make it challenging to incorporate Orff Schulwerk ideas in the field of instrument instruction. Learning and playing an instrument was historically never a main curricular subject in European educational systems. The use of musical instruments belonged to the area of handicrafts and guilds. The professional musicians of a town hall in Germany, for example, the so-called *Stadtpfeifer*, were part of the guild system, along with other craftsmen such as carpenters and shoemakers. The rules of music making and teaching methods obeyed the rules of the guild and were protected as guild secrets. They were passed on from master to apprentice in a personal and unwritten way. Therefore, published methods for instrument teaching appeared very late in history. These historic facts have consequences, i.e., viewing music-making as a handicraft always puts the music in the center of the teaching process. Even more precisely, the technical realization of music on the particular instrument is the focus. Pedagogical issues and the student as a person were of minor importance. The apprentice had to subordinate to the musical and instrumental laws and necessities. It is remarkable that this master—apprentice model continued in the conservatories in a changed society of the 19th century. Even today it is not difficult to find relics of this traditional craftsmanship-oriented thinking.

Examples of old-style or traditional instrument instruction:

1. In learning to play an instrument there are (sometimes exclusively) technical problems and musical questions to be solved. A musical piece counts as achieved when all technical problems are mastered.
2. Achieving a high level of professional competence is an ultimate objective. Therefore, there is always the demand for "faster" and "more difficult"—the next piece always has to be more challenging than the one before. The literature chosen by the teacher can be felt as a permanently ascending staircase. Completed music is soon put aside and forgotten because it no longer represents the actual technical level of the student.
3. In periodic recitals, students must prove their competence, performing the most recently studied composition, which is of course the most demanding one. This practice in many music schools and conservatories is even more questionable if we ask: What professional musician would risk going on stage with his last studied and most demanding piece? More likely is that she would study it, leave it to rest for a certain time, and after a new phase of practicing, add it to her concert repertoire. But for her students, this professionally and psychologically explainable procedure is invalid. The student has—sometimes under stress and fear of failure—to survive the presentation on stage. No wonder that a great number of students do not tolerate this pressure and they stop their instrument instruction. The lasting memory of such an experience is of disappointment and failure.

To all these aspects comes one more example, which shows even the greatest distance between traditional instrument instruction and the intentions of the Orff Schulwerk:

4. Before students receive their first lessons, in many schools they must pass an entrance exam. It has to be proven that the investment on instrument instruction is justified. This procedure can be understood if there is a long waiting list. But easily this entrance exam degenerates to "fishing for talent." It is especially appealing for all those instrument teachers who evaluate their professional success primarily on how many students they have led to professional careers. They draw the simple conclusion: "Good students" means "good teacher." Question: What teacher in a primary school could permit such a simplistic and one-dimensional conclusion?

We have to be fair and admit that a great number of instrument teachers distance themselves from this strict tradition, but it is remarkable in how many places this practice still exists unquestioned. The Orff Schulwerk does not have space in that world. It would only hamper the speed of technical progress because of eating up too much time.

At first glance the two concepts "learning an instrument" and the "Orff Schulwerk approach" seem to be incompatible. Orff Schulwerk encourages a playful and experimental interaction with an instrument. Traditional instrument instruction, on the other hand, puts from the beginning the indispensable need for proper technique in the center. Consequently, if we want to implement the philosophy of the Orff Schulwerk in instrument teaching, we have to find a solution that incorporates the intentions of the Orff Schulwerk as well as the technical demands of instrument playing without restricting the core and basic necessities of either.

Some clear rules may help to accomplish this goal:

a. In order to respect the technical necessities, Orff Schulwerk has to operate in areas where it does not negatively affect the production of a correct sound, or—ideally—where it can support it.

b. As previously explained, traditional instrument instruction that is concerned first and foremost with the student advancing in the shortest time to the highest technical level would see the Orff Schulwerk as an unnecessary obstacle. But instrument teachers who put the student, the musician, i.e., the human being, in the center of the work, will find a great partner in the Orff Schulwerk. They will encourage and teach their students not only to interpret high quality music well, but also to create their own music. They will use improvisation and composition as enrichment in their lessons, as an activity that is complementary to the study of composed music.

Seeing instrument teaching in this way requires a different approach to thinking about and preparing the class. Improvisation, as all creative activities, needs time and patience. It requests the right to assume risks, even to commit mistakes. And mistakes in improvisation have a different meaning. A wrong note in classical music interpretation is a recognizable error, a flaw, a contaminant of a piece of art. In improvisation, however, a note that sticks out because it does not fit into the tonality or the musical context is a step in the experience of advancing one's own musical expression. Mistakes in improvisation do not have so much of a poisoning effect; they are easily excused. We know the informal code of jazz musicians: "If you make a mistake, do it twice"—i.e., by repeating an unwanted sound you make it appear intentional and interesting, even provoking. It will not always help, but it explains that mistakes are unavoidable incidents in improvisation, and they help the student musician to gain experience. And sometimes they even lead into a more interesting direction.

What does it mean when we say we "play an instrument?" Do we really "play" when we are operating an instrument and making it sound? We often think of play as something not serious or frivolous or easy. It seems not to be the proper word for that what we do with our instrument. *Sonare* in Italian and *tocar* in Spanish make it more understandable. But they refer only to the physical process of making an instrument sound. To "play an instrument," however, (like *spielen* in German or *jouer* in French and in several other languages) points to more than just the acoustical action.

By all the vast quantity of definitions connected with the word "play" we find a common thread: to play means to have the freedom to decide and act within a structure that is clearly defined by rules. It is easily explained if we look to the world of sport, especially to ball games, like football, basketball, or tennis. There are clear and strict rules, but from the moment the ball begins to move, the decisive element is in the spontaneous decisions of the players. This way of "playing" is "improvising" in its purest sense, even if it is not named so.

In music we may connect this form of playing (improvising) with a jazz musician, who displays his freedom over a defined system of chords and scales. In folk music, something similar may happen. Even the printed "rules" of a sophisticated score of a Beethoven sonata still give a certain freedom that allows different interpretations of such a masterpiece.

But with these examples we face the main problem: In music we connect this interaction between rules and playful freedom with skillfulness and expertise. Improvisation is only allowed for musicians who dominate their instrument perfectly and know the rules. For the others, improvisation does not exist—and many professional musicians are so exclusively specialized in playing written music, that they do not even miss it.

A solution that could include improvisation and creativity in general instrument teaching would need to divide the teaching time (of one student) into two different levels, making a clear difference in the degrees of technical difficulty. We call it here the "pioneer level" and the "play level."

Pioneer level
Here the student faces new challenges in order to improve technical playing skills. Also, different musical forms and historic styles are discussed and applied. It is exactly what traditional instrument instruction does exclusively.

Play level
Here the technical demand is lower, giving the freedom to deal with the musical material in a creative way, to improvise, and to make up one's own music, i.e., "to play."

To explain this concept, we will use a fragment of piece No. 10 from the *Klavierübung* by Carl Orff (1934a, p. 6).

10

fine

with kind permission of Schott Music

There are two ways to categorize it:

1. The student is a beginner, technically ready to study this music. The piece would then be used for work at the "pioneer level."
2. The student can easily master the piece and is able to play it almost prima vista. The piece would be material to play with. The teacher invites the student to find his own modifications and helps him to include his own ideas that personalize the piece. It will become his own piece.

The starting point of this process could be to establish the basic line and harmonic structure that appears four times (only slightly varied in the melody of every fourth bar).

The next step is to modify the short melody line by changing the rhythm and/or pitches while keeping the basic integrity of the line:

A next step is to fill in the first and fifth bars (empty below)…

…with notes that lead logically to the main motif. To focus, the teacher suggests solutions using four 8th notes, as follows:

(Later more complex rhythmic formulas can lead to a dizzying array of possible solutions.)

This proposal to find different solutions for a basic idea (you have to lead to the g with four 8th notes) is along the same lines as the "Ostinato exercises for tuned percussion instruments" in *Orff-Schulwerk* Volume I (Orff & Keetman [Murray], 1958, p. 82).

This approach to improvisation has its roots in the Renaissance practice of decoration of the third (found in *Orff-Schulwerk* Volume IV) and the Baroque practice of melodic ornamentation (found often in the Sarabandes of Bach's English Suites, for example). The following example is an excerpt from a 1752 treatise on how to play the flute by Johann Joachim Quantz (1697–1773). The example shows ways to create variations on three quarter notes using the pitch c.

The little example above by Carl Orff, with its simple structure and limited technical problems, invites students to experience the creation of their own music, to improvise and/ or compose new variations at their highest level of technical skill and understanding. This is precisely a central objective of the Orff Schulwerk. If we imagine further that there would be space in the instrumental music class to include movement and dance in the teaching process, then we would further achieve the concept of Carl Orff's elemental music education.

With regard to all good pedagogical ideas and all attempts to introduce the concept of Orff Schulwerk into the teaching of musical instruments, we cannot ignore the ambiguous position of instrument instruction: It is still standing between pedagogy and handicraft. On one side, it should be part of music education in general, but it also wants to fulfill its role as a starting point for the training of a professional musician. Both areas cannot at all be regarded as identical and the ambiguity may bring a certain pressure to teacher and student. It may be a common goal to gain a playing competence as high as possible. The admiration of the star instrumentalists, known through recordings and other media, may be a motivational device for both professional and amateur aspirations. But there are different objectives that demand different strategies and assessment criteria.

These parallel worlds of musician craftsperson and music educator can cause identity problems for the teacher. Because of her training in the conservatory, she feels that she is a musician, very often with scarce or no pedagogic preparation. She may see herself as a performing artist according to the content of her studies. However, a career on stage might have been too risky, and she has to teach for economic reasons. From this point of view, it might seem that the instrument teacher has a lower social/professional status than a "real" musician!

In fact, this should be understood the other way round, or at least without any comparison. An instrument teacher with pedagogic studies has not only a performance competence but also a teaching competence. Being able to play an instrument—and it may even be masterly—does not guarantee effective and successful teaching. It is well known that if instrument teachers have difficulties, it is seldom because of lack of technical competence, but more often because they are not able to connect positively with their students. This is not surprising. A good mathematician is not always a good mathematics teacher and there are history teachers who would do better in the archives of a museum than in a classroom.

There is another remarkable characteristic of instrument teachers. Teachers in all other fields of education are normally specialized with regard to a certain age or developmental level of their students (kindergarten, primary school, secondary school, special needs, etc.). Teachers of a musical instrument are not classified by age group or level—they are qualified for all ages and levels. But does an instrument teacher always have the gift and the flexibility to respond in an adequate pedagogic way to students from the age of primary school beginners up to young graduates? Does it not show again that in instrument instruction, the music is typically put in the center and not the student?

To summarize, Orff Schulwerk and instrument instruction have a very delicate, or better, difficult relationship. Orff Schulwerk however can have its place and be an enrichment in instrumental music instruction if it respects and responds to the peculiarities of this teaching area. Challenged to think beyond the notes and make the music truly their own, the students are then on the way of really playing when they play their instruments. They will certainly appreciate it.

CHAPTER 11
Orff Schulwerk Today

More than 70 years have passed since the Orff Schulwerk premiered on air, opening new ways to approach music actively and with creativity. It was a small start, but with far-reaching repercussions. Today Orff Schulwerk can be experienced in many places all over the world. Teachers from the Orff Institute in Salzburg, Austria have traveled world-wide to offer courses and workshops, and many of the international graduates from the Orff Institute have returned to their countries and formed work groups to convey and practice Orff Schulwerk. At present Orff Schulwerk associations exist in more than 40 countries where members organize training courses and weekend seminars for teachers. They provide assistance in understanding the goals of the Schulwerk and putting them into practice. It is important that these training programs both convey the intentions of Orff and Keetman (see the "Principles of Orff Schulwerk" in Chapter 6) and also take the sociocultural situation of the respective country into account (i.e., including in their program songs, dances, stories, and poems of their own cultural heritage). A great number of these Orff Schulwerk associations keep contact with the Carl Orff Foundation,[1] the legal successor of Carl Orff that holds the rights of his artistic, pedagogical, and philosophical oeuvre. Representatives of these Orff Schulwerk associations gather annually for an active exchange on educational and artistic questions with the International Orff-Schulwerk Forum Salzburg (IOSFS).[2] This "Forum" is a platform of experts in close local and professional relationship to the Carl Orff Institute[3] of the University of Music "Mozarteum" in Salzburg, Austria. IOSFS is the successor organization of the *Zentralstelle für das Orff-Schulwerk*, which was founded under the guidance of Carl Orff in 1961 along with the Carl Orff Institute. Another important institution bearing Orff's name is the Orff Zentrum München[4] a place for research, documentation, and information about the composer and pedagogue. It is a Bavarian State Institute, founded in order to archive, administer, and keep alive the voluminous artistic legacy of Carl Orff.

It is not easy to assess worldwide the actual place of the Orff Schulwerk in music and dance education. The situation from one country to another is too different. There are places where the Schulwerk still has the aura of something new, is still modern, even taken as trendy. In some places "Orff" stands for no less than modern music pedagogy and finds growing interest. But this tendency needs to be observed very closely in order to avoid commercial development of the Schulwerk in a way that can no longer be harmonized with Orff and Keetman's core intentions.

The situation is very different in those countries that came in contact with Orff Schulwerk from the beginning (in the early 1950s). Of course, this is especially valid for Germany itself. In that context I remember a conference during the 1990s in Germany to which experts were

---

1 https://www.orff.de
2 https://www.orff-schulwerk-forum-salzburg.org
3 https://www.orff.moz.ac.at
4 https://www.ozm.bayern.de

invited to present all music pedagogical concepts that were used then in German schools. Hermann Regner, the former director of the Carl Orff Institute and at that time acting president of the Carl Orff Foundation, asked me to speak about the Schulwerk during this convention. When it was my turn to start with my report and I began with "Hartmann—Orff Schulwerk" came the spontaneous reply by the presenter, "Orff Schulwerk—does it still exist?" Leaving it open whether it was a remark of genuine surprise or just a jocular jibe, it brings us to different conclusions:

a. If you connect the expression "Orff Schulwerk" first, even exclusively, with the initial radio programs and the almost simultaneously published five volumes of *Musik für Kinder* (Music for Children), then nearly five decades later the Orff Schulwerk really could be called antiquated, even historic.
b. In the textbooks for music education in primary schools in the German speaking areas (Germany, Austria, and a part of Switzerland) you hardly find one that does not refer at least in part to creative and movement oriented Schulwerk ideas (very often even without mentioning expressively the origin). Hence it can be concluded that Carl Orff has achieved his central pedagogical objective, meaning that the integration of the children's creativity in music making, dancing, and speech, has found its place in schools. No need any more for the Schulwerk itself!

But this statement should not be accepted for reality. In places where the Orff Schulwerk has found its place in the normal curriculum, a permanent control is necessary in order to prevent the Schulwerk from becoming a school subject that is restricted by school norms, which would destroy its very essence. He warned in 1963: "The so-called 'Orff instruments' are being used in many schools today, but it would be a mistake to conclude that Schulwerk has a solid foundation in all these schools" (Carl Orff, 2011b/1964, p. 152).

In principle we have to recognize that there is a certain tension between Schulwerk and school reality. On one side is the creativity with all its necessary freedoms and on the other side are the essential didactic obligations and constraints surrounding each particular situation (strict timetable, assessment norms, the curriculum with clearly defined teaching content). To bring both sides into a working relationship—even harmonizing together—is not an easy task. Reconciling the two sides of this challenge was left by the initiators of the Schulwerk for each teacher who wants to work in the style of the Orff Schulwerk to determine. Therefore, it depends on the professional competence of every teacher to decide if this lack of official methodical guidance should be seen as a weakness or as a challenge and feature of personal freedom and responsibility.

The Orff Schulwerk has gotten on in years, but there are no signs of it being old. The "roots" of our Schulwerk tree still provide the "branches" with vigor and energy and if we understand its intentions correctly and consequently put them into practice, then Carl Orff and Gunild Keetman's pedagogical oeuvre is as fresh, exciting, and important today as it was on the day of its first presentation on the radio.

EXTENSIONS

Throughout the previous chapters, there have been numerous references to improvisation and composition. Here we take a look at these important themes more closely, both theoretically and with examples from my own experience. The original texts are two articles that were published in 2010[1] and 2012[2] in *Orff-Schulwerk Informationen*, periodical of the Orff Institute of "Mozarteum," University of Music in Salzburg, Austria and the International Orff-Schulwerk Forum Salzburg.

---

1 *Orff-Schulwerk Informationen 83* (Summer 2010), pp. 7–12.
2 *Orff-Schulwerk Informationen 86* (Summer 2012), pp. 7–9.

Extension One
Considerations about Improvisation in Orff Schulwerk

Probably the most notable innovation offered to school music education with the second birth of Orff Schulwerk in the radio programs was the focus on improvisation. Placing improvisation at the center of a music lesson demands a very particular teaching and working style. In the earlier work at the Günther-Schule, there were adult students and teachers who were open to experimentation, and indeed, were attracted to the school because of the freedom to create that it offered.

In 1948, however, the situation was different. This new pedagogical concept was now to be adapted to the public school system, precisely to the primary school. It was not understood as obligatory, but it was presented in a way that made it clear that improvisation should be seriously considered. Therefore, it is not surprising that the approach to music offered by the Schulwerk did not immediately evoke unbridled enthusiasm. Walter Panofsky, who provided the principal impetus to this new radio program, reported the reaction of a select group of pedagogues to the first radio program:

> It became apparent that most of the teachers considered Orff's ideas revolutionary; they were close to Pestalozzi's and meant an introduction to music through music, and that a child's own creative powers be awakened principally by other children and not by the authority of the teacher. A few of the teachers received the idea enthusiastically, but the majority adhered to the traditional principles of rational education. (Panofsky, 1962, p. 71)

Luckily, there was a fundamental change in the reception of the Schulwerk in the years that followed. In the past seven decades, Orff Schulwerk programs have flourished in schools worldwide. In any case, it can be stated that the particularly delicate relationship between improvisation and school still exists today. Even when teachers express a positive opinion towards improvisation, there still remain the doubts about how to put this risky activity into practice.

In this context I remember a situation during a lesson in my class called "Introduction to instrumental and vocal pedagogy" at the University of Music in Vienna. It was a conversation about improvisation in the class on instrumental instruction. Even before going into details, I wanted to know from the students—future instrument teachers—what was their personal relationship to improvisation on their instrument. The answers were like this:

A cellist remarked: *Improvisation?—Ok, sometimes when I am alone at home and practice, once in a while I just play along just for me. But this I do only for myself.*

A double bass player from the jazz department showed surprise: *Playing music without improvisation?—I cannot imagine that. Improvisation is for me "the gate to music."*

A flutist: *I mean, it's super if someone improvises well. But this also you have to learn seriously. You would need a teacher for that.*

It could be that my introductory words had already showed my positive opinion about improvisation. Maybe it helped that the answers were generally positive, though sometimes with a certain distance. A recorder student said very enthusiastically, *Last year I went for an improvisation course in England. The teacher said, "Just play along!" It was fantastic!* Finally, a pianist from a former Eastern Bloc country gave this categorical answer: *In our conservatory improvisation was forbidden.* Silence, astonishment, slight bafflement, and suppressed laughter came from the others. But perhaps there was also a note of understanding on the part of her colleagues, because improvisation is not only appealing, but also risky and unpredictable as the name indicates. Improvisation needs time and contains a quality that we know from other areas of life—appeal and risk are very often close together.

Improvisation implies the unknown, stands for freedom, and accepts open results. To a certain degree it eludes a planning control. The Schulwerk had something provoking when it was presented the first time to a broader group of teachers. So, no wonder it had difficulties gaining ground in the school system.

Consequently, misunderstandings were unavoidable. The models in the Schulwerk were thought of as finished results. They appeared in print like little music pieces, and they sounded like that. Keetman and Orff did not want to hide their mastery by writing them down. It made them attractive just to play them as written. After all, it follows the same line of conventional music understanding, to play compositions as they are written. But the central concern of the Schulwerk, i.e., to create one's own music, got completely lost.

In my time as a teacher in Munich at a primary school with emphasis on music (a so-called *Orff-Modellschule*), I sometimes liked to present one of the volume pieces just as written. Because improvisation and creative music making had a large space in my music lesson, I saw it as legitimate to do so. It also gave a chance to show the children how nicely these pieces were made. This brought me into the following situation: First, we were learning the melody of the piece (*Orff-Schulwerk* Volume II, page 14, No. 2), working with musical question-and-answer games. The discussion started when I intended to work on the accompanying ostinato. Obviously, this was not as attractive as the melody and so the question appeared: "Why do we need to play that after we are able to play the melody?" And then more decisively: "Why don't we do something of our own?" I tried to give an explanation like the one mentioned before: "The pieces in this book are so beautiful that it is sometimes worth taking one of them as it is written." The reaction was mixed and so after a short discussion we decided to continue with two separate groups.

Luckily, we had two connected rooms at our disposal. One group (approximately half) remained with me and the other group went to the second room and tried to find their own accompaniment connected with the earlier elaborated melody. At the end of the lesson, we shared our results. We deliberately tried to avoid comparing and we approved both versions. Some weeks later, when we were planning the repertoire for a parents' meeting, we came again to this issue: What version of the piece should we choose? After a short discussion: Both.

On one side I have to confess secretly that my teacher's soul felt a short pinch when the children were questioning my proposal. But it was only short! Of course, on the other (bigger!) side I was glad to see how self-confident my students were. Finally, it was the outcome of a teaching style that gave the freedom for improvisation and invited them to develop their individual creativity.

If we accept that music education is not only "education to music" but also includes "education through music," then the focus on improvisation provides rich material for educational work. The students will recognize that their own ideas are welcomed. They are allowed to decide and receive a certain freedom, but they also take responsibility. At the same time, teachers learn to allow this freedom and to grant partnership with their students by doing so.

When improvisation is applied at school it has to be seen from two different perspectives: On the one hand there is the artistic role of improvisation. The musician chooses a theme, takes a melody or a harmony as a basis and develops the music out of the moment. For the musician Orff, this was "an essential constituent of his artistic craft" (Kugler, 2000, p. 244). On the other hand, improvisation has a didactic function; it can be used as a methodic device. Independent of the subject, improvisation can be seen as a type of discovery learning, i.e., the student gains experience by doing something that afterwards can be transformed in reflected knowledge. "Experience before sight before theory" it might be called by Gordon's Music Learning Theory pedagogy (Bluestine, 2000).

This brings the teacher to a twofold difficulty:

a. Allowing the students freedom for artistic decisions, which is only possible with a teaching style far from any authoritarian impulses.
b. Maintaining a certain leadership so that the learning process does not get lost in randomness and indifference, and also acting very sensitively and not manipulating the students to pre-planned results.

We can conclude that Orff Schulwerk needs teachers who have experienced the excitement of improvisation for themselves. But for putting it in a sensitive and pedagogic way into classroom practice this is not enough. Do the Schulwerk volumes give help and advice?

Opening the first volume, in the foreword it reads, "*Music for Children* has grown out of work with children," stating then that the limitation to the pentatonic scale would correspond to the mentality of small children "to express themselves easily" (Orff & Keetman [Murray], 1958, Foreword). Advice and comments for specific working steps and even the term "improvisation" are completely absent. Only in part two of the first volume (Rhythmic and Melodic Exercises) are there some simple suggestions for improvising melodies and for ideas to continue to complete rhythmic phrases by improvisation.

Orff and Keetman did not regard this lack of further information as an omission, taking into account in what context these five central volumes had been published. At that time, it was no more than a compilation of musical material for an educational radio program. The five volumes contained nothing more than *possible* final results of processes of improvisation that were explained more in detail on the radio and presented with children making music. The explanation in Carl Orff's own words: "So the Schulwerk is a collection of models that seek on inverted paths to lead from where they have come, to improvisation" (Orff, 2013/1932-33, p. 166). For the listeners and users of the radio program this point of view made sense. The printed material was understandable and could be used in the classroom following the hints that came through the loudspeaker.

But it was different for people who got these volumes in their hands without the opportunity of hearing the radio programs. Something occurred regarding what Hans Bergese had expressed back in 1937 in a letter to Carl Orff. He complained that the music teachers would not understand that "the Schulwerk is actually anti-print, that it is an idea of style, a way of working that one can teach but cannot describe" (Kugler, 2013b/2002, p. 99). "Anti-print" – this expression describes exactly the whole difficulty of inserting the pedagogical concept of Orff Schulwerk into our culture, which is based on the written word. Orff Schulwerk evades the written permanence in a comparable way to ethnic music and the early epoch of European art music (Kugler).

Finally, the difficulties listed here have led to the high number of publications and countless teacher training programs for the purpose of explaining and practicing the relevant teaching techniques that are appropriate for Orff Schulwerk:

- As early as 1949 Gunild Keetman began offering courses for children at *Mozarteum Salzburg* (the University for Music and Dramatic Arts at Salzburg) accompanied by training programs for teachers. This time, dance was given the appropriate importance, which previously could not be served in print or in the purely auditory radio productions.
- Wilhelm Keller published his *Introduction to Music for Children* in 1954, which he republished in an amended and expanded form in 1963. Here also we see the first cautious didactical steps, i.e., content is put in a sequential order and duration of working periods are proposed.[1] Here, for the first time, there are detailed suggestions on how to deal with the demand for improvisation.
- Gunild Keetman's *Elementaria: First Acquaintance with Orff-Schulwerk* was first published in 1970 (1974 in English) and is described as "a practical and essential guide for educationalists concerned with Orff Schulwerk." (From review on www.amazon.com)
- Michael Kugler's (2000) comparative study of the Jaques-Dalcroze method and the Orff Schulwerk *Elementare Musikübung* offers more profound analyses of the musical material as well as the connected working style.

How did Carl Orff and Gunild Keetman present the idea of improvisation in their radio program? The first broadcast[2] is only an introductory meeting. The children, who had never seen a xylophone, began to tentatively play and sing two-tone melodies. Speaking to the extremely shy studio children, the presenter Rudolf Kirmeyer said, "Children, today we still need the musicians. But within a short time, we will not need them anymore; we will play ourselves and make music."

In the second program, the first decisive step toward improvisation was made. After the children were familiarized with songs on a three-tone scale, one of the children was asked to come to a glockenspiel. He was invited to find his own sequence with the metal bars lying on the instrument. More children followed and improvised their individual solutions. The presenter endorsed every child, sometimes gently improving rhythmic incorrectness. He himself even proposed sequences that went away from the familiar way to use the three-tone scale e–g–a (asking them to end the melody with the a).

Improvisation signifies the opportunity to move freely within a given framework, i.e., one improvises on a theme. Just to play along is only one of the options—in a certain sense the exception to the rule. Only the security of knowing the rules of the game creates the ease that is crucial for any improvisation. The Schulwerk offers this framework through…

a. … limited and therefore easily manageable scale material (which can be augmented over time).

b. … simple rhythmic building blocks and four-bar phrase structures that are typical in our traditional occidental music.

For teachers of today, this framework, which offers the urtext of the Schulwerk, may be viewed as too narrow. Even if we sing predominantly tonal songs with children in an early

---

1 This was an indispensable step to help teachers incorporate Schulwerk in the school curriculum (even when Orff and especially Werner Thomas saw didactics having too close a school-like diluting effect).

2 The radio broadcasts are in the archive of the *Bayerischer Rundfunk, München* (Bavarian Radio, Munich).

childhood music class, we also include singing storytelling, which gives total tonal freedom. The musical language of today includes sounds that can no longer be set in pentagram lines. A teaching practice that understands itself as being in the Orff Schulwerk tradition will also include ideas from Gertrud Meyer-Denkmann, Lilli Friedemann, and George Selfe, to name just some of the ones who amplified the tonal repertoire in music education. Also, the findings from Edwin Gordon's research may be included.

This process that broadened the sound spectrum for Schulwerk activities was also discussed inside the "Orff-World." For the teachers at the Orff Institute, it became clear after a while that the five volumes of *Music for Children* were not the end of the matter, but the beginning—a point of departure for further development. The development of contemporary musical language had to be taken in account. Examples of publications with special regard to improvisation can be found by Wilhelm Keller (1973), in the essays of Ernst Wieblitz (1978), and in Hermann Regner's *Chorstudien* (1976). Further examples of how Orff and Keetman's pedagogical concepts were adapted concerning the temporal and cultural reality were the *Music for Children—Orff Schulwerk*, American Edition (Regner, 1977–1982) and the material for early childhood music education *Musik und Tanz für Kinder* (Haselbach, Nykrin, & Regner, 1996). As the Schulwerk spread worldwide, *Music for Children* volumes were adapted using rhymes and folk material from other countries—Argentina, Brazil, Ghana, Japan, China, and more. Also bridges to Jazz have been built (*Now's the Time*, Doug Goodkin)

Orff Schulwerk has brought improvisation into the school. As it gives importance to the ideas of the students, at the same time it reduces the typical school 'ping-pong' mechanism of question (always the teacher) and answer (always the student), always in the frame of right or wrong. Improvisation gives freedom.

Extension Two
Considerations about Students' Composition in Orff Schulwerk

At first glance, improvisation and composition seem to be two opposing processes. While the first just "happens," it gives the feeling of lightness, even fleetingness and randomness. It places the process of making spontaneous music in the center. The second, in contrast, is connected with meticulous planning and construction. It is marked by the will to create something consistent, at least something that survives beyond the mere act of playing. It implies intellectual work and expert knowledge. Finally, it leads to written notation that preserves and communicates further than the moment of conception.

This bipolarity and interrelatedness that represent improvisation and composition within the Schulwerk were intended from the beginning. Apart from improvisation games already in the first run of the radio programs, the children were encouraged to write down their own little compositions. We can imagine that the primarily intention was to learn how to write down music. But it also corresponds to the idea of creating a small composition to express something personal that can be communicated to others.

The topic of children's compositions has been written about in several articles in the *Orff-Schulwerk Informationen*, the magazine of the Orff Institute and the International Orff-Schulwerk Forum Salzburg. Ernst Wieblitz (1987): "Composing for self-made instruments;" Ulrike Jungmair (1996): "Let's compose something;" and Leonardo Riveiro Holgado (2007): "From building instruments to elemental composition" all shed light on this important subject.

If we go into more detail about the nature and importance of elemental composition, it is necessary to clarify some questions:

• What is the meaning of elemental composition?
• What can and what do children actually want to compose?
• What help can the teacher contribute without interfering too much in the creative process?
• What musical language can be used by the children?

What is the meaning of elemental composition?
It is best to ask Carl Orff himself. In his oftentimes quoted article "Orff-Schulwerk – Past and Future" he writes:

> *Elemental music is never music alone but forms a unity with movement, dance, and speech. It is music that one makes oneself, in which one takes part not as a listener but as a participant. It is unsophisticated, employs no big forms and no big architectural structures, and it uses small sequence forms, ostinato, and rondo. Elemental music is near the earth, natural, physical, within the range of everyone to learn it and to experience it, and suitable for the child.* (Orff, 2011b/1964, p. 144)

This lets us understand elemental composition as creating music that can be done by children under the careful guidance of a teacher, or even without help. The musical result should be something the children can identify with, a music they understand. In this aspect, rehearsing is a form of shaping their own ideas—it is not just a formal act of learning. Then it is of minor importance whether the composition is kept by writing it down, by electronic recording, or by memory.

What can and what do children actually want to compose?

The model pieces of the Schulwerk offer examples of how children can create little rondos or other simple forms with ostinato, provided that in doing so there is the guiding hand of a teacher. So music for children will become music by children. In addition, other starting points like graphic notation are possible. Wilhelm Keller did pioneer work in that subject with the volumes of *Ludi Musici* (1973–1975).

During my entire professional career, I have been interested in finding out what music children would produce if left alone—a music that is more than just the joy of sound-making. We know that children can do their own painting without any adult help. And we also know that children's paintings can be very expressive. Why does this creativity not happen in music in the same way?

One of the reasons might be that traditional music (and this also includes children's songs and dances) uses fixed and unalterable parameters from the beginning. It is the pitch and rhythm based on a steady pulse. Any deviation from these two parameters is easy to recognize and diminishes the musical quality. The visual arts also have these strict parameters: proportion and perspective. But luckily, they are not applied to children's creations. In a picture, it is no problem if a man standing next to his house is almost double the size of the building! This shows the creative freedom that children are missing in (traditional) music. Sound creations that leave exact tonal pitch and steady pulse out of consideration would be the equivalent to children's painting.

To find an answer on how children's own music sounds, sometimes I observed the children in a music and movement class, alone or with my conservatory students. Pretending that the lesson had not yet started, "because I had to put some papers in order," I left them alone with the instruments without guidance. After a short time of individual experimenting where the students were just trying out and interchanging different instruments (not always without conflict), they started to make musical contact with the others. Interesting proposals to make up some music together were discussed. Then came ideas like this: "I am going to play up [a scale on a xylophone] and then you do something [with a triangle]. And then I play down again." This was tried out, repeated, and afterwards came the change of the instruments. There were no sequences of parallel thirds; it was not about a beautiful sound. It was mostly about structures and playing rules that were understandable and acceptable for all.

After those moments of observing, it was sometimes even possible for me to include these structures in our work. It helped us to construct a longer piece. Having these experiences in mind, Orff's visionary phrases do not sound idealistically exaggerated:

> *Musical instruction for a child does not begin in the music lesson. Playtime is the starting point. One should not come to music—it should arise of itself. What is important is that the child is allowed to play, undisturbed, expressing the internal externally.* (Orff, 2011a/1932, p. 68)

An even more striking result came in one of my classes showing how art, story, and music can join in the child's imagination. It took place during the time I was a teacher at a so-called *Orff-Modellschule* in Munich in Germany. The children were given the task of drawing a picture or a sketch and then translating it into music. One group of four 10-year-old children came up with the following picture:

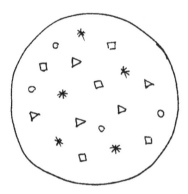

The realization in sound emerged after lengthy discussion and much rehearsal. Over an ostinato of heavy strokes on a large drum (the circle!), two glockenspiels and one xylophone played short melodic ostinato phrases. After the children had presented their piece to the rest of the class, they described it thus: "The circle is the wall of a (medieval) town, and the towers are present in the drumbeats. They guard the children who are playing in the town."

Although this piece did not use conventional material, the other children asked to hear it several times. They simply felt that this was an expression of their world: the big city, their own feelings, their search for security. (Hartmann, 2000, p. 95)

What help can the teacher contribute without interfering too much in the creative process?
To release the creative impulse, the attitude of the teacher is vital, and the preparation of appropriate material is equally important. When we look into the volumes, we see in the music pieces possible results of musical processes as they could have happened in the imaginations of Orff and Keetman. In this sense the teacher should have possible results in mind, but NOT with the intention of implementing them exactly. It would be against the principle of creativity. The ideas of the teacher should serve as a dormant reserve in case the students need help or inspiration. If the teacher were to promote personal ideas too much, the students would quickly give up their own still vague ideas and with that their competence to decide and work out their own plans. After all, they are used to that in other learning situations and in other subjects. In order to allow the children to share their ideas, elemental composition depends a lot on the self-control of the teacher and the discipline to not interfere too early or too much.

What musical language can be used?
Regarding the musical language that the children may use, there are two basic options:

a. The traditional scale-oriented and metric music
b. Playing with free sounds

Of course, combinations of both are possible.

The music of our time includes infinite possibilities of sound. But the musical language with clear parameters of pentatonic, diatonic, or chromatic scales and time structures based on pulse is still standard. It is valid not only in traditional art music, but also in folk and pop.

Therefore, the dominance of these sounds in the school environment is only natural. Yet it can be problematic in the case of musical creations that use familiar metric and scale-oriented devices because there may be an audible gap between the intentions of the children and the resulting realization. As explained before, we would hear the difference between correct and flawed, the shortcomings in pitch and rhythm.

Creating music with free metric sequences and undetermined scales opens more alternatives to the traditional style. We can use graphic notation, programmatic sounds, and accompaniment to a scene or a story. Of course, even when there is more freedom accepted, we still can recognize differences in quality that can be improved. But who expects perfection from the children?

Whatever musical language the children use for their own compositions—traditionally-oriented or unconventional—the music is different from the music that is heard in a concert or in the media. Children do not come with the idea to compete. Nor do they do so with their paintings and other works of art. But we can assume that children who make up their own music, or at least are actively included in the process of inventing music, will listen more consciously and with more "open ears" to music that is composed by others.

No matter from which side we may approach the Orff Schulwerk—using improvisation, composition, dance improvisation, or one's own choreography—in the center is always the creativity of the students. Orff and Keetman remind us of that again and again. They don't make it easy for us, however, because their models of musical pieces are so artful and attractive. Even as they invite us just to play them, they should guide us to our own music.

CHRONOLOGY

The following timeline shows only the dates in the lives of Carl Orff and Gunild Keetman that refer directly or indirectly to the development of Orff Schulwerk, compared with a synchronized compilation of relevant information.

	Carl Orff		Gunild Keetman		
1895	Carl Orff born in Munich on 10 July				
				1902	E. Jaques-Dalcroze starts to present his music pedagogical reform ideas in courses
		1904	Gunild Doris Keetman born in Wuppertal-Elberfeld on 5 June		
1910	First compositions for voice and piano			1910 to 1914	E. Jaques-Dalcroze's school for Music and Rhythm at Dresden-Hellerau
1912 to 1914	Studies at the "Akademie der Tonkunst," Munich			1914 to 1918	World War I
1924	Founding and organization of the Günther-Schule, institution for gymnastic, rhythmic, music, and dance	1924 to 1925	Orienting studies of History of Art and Music (Bonn) and Physical Education (Berlin)	1925	The main principles of the Kodály concept are formed
		1926 to 1928	Studies at Günther-Schule, encounter with Carl Orff, Dorothee Günther, Maja Lex		
		1928 to 1944	Teacher at Günther-Schule		
1931 to 1934	Publication of a first Schulwerk-Edition: Orff-Schulwerk, Elementare Musikübung	1931 to 1934	Publication of a first Schulwerk-Edition: Orff-Schulwerk, Elementare Musikübung		
1932	Collaboration with Leo Kestenberg				
				1935	Z. Kódály and Jenó Ádám start a music pedagogical reform project with new curriculum and new teaching techniques
		1936	Composes music for the opening performance of the 11th Olympic Games in Berlin		
1937	Premiere of Carmina Burana, Frankfurt a. Main, 8 June				

	Carl Orff		Gunild Keetman		
				1938	C. E. Seashore, *Psychology of Music*
				1939 to 1945	World War II
1948	Start of Orff Schulwerk broadcasts on Bavarian Radio on 15 September	1948	Start of Orff Schulwerk broadcasts on Bavarian Radio on 15 September		
		1949	*Die Weihnachtsgeschichte* (Text Carl Orff) Orff Schulwerk children's courses at the Mozarteum Academy Salzburg		
1950 to 1954	Publication of the five volumes *Orff-Schulwerk—Music for Children*	1950 to 1954	Publication of the five volumes *Orff-Schulwerk—Music for Children*		
		1957 to 1958	Television recordings of Orff Schulwerk in Munich (together with Godela Orff		
1961	Founding of the Orff Institute, Central Office and Seminar of the Mozarteum Academy	1961 to 1966	Teacher and shared Directorship with Carl Orff and Wilhelm Keller at Orff Institute	1965	Edwin Gordon, the Musical Aptitude Profile
1963	Official opening of the new building of the Orff Institute in Salzburg	1962 to 1980	Journeys to represent Orff Schulwerk internationally (some together with Carl Orff) to Canada, Japan, Belgium, Switzerland, Italy, UK, Senegal, Egypt, France, Spain, Denmark, Israel		
1982	Carl Orff dies on 29 March in Munich. He is buried in a chapel next to the Church of the Monastery Andechs				
		1990	Gunild Keetman dies on 14 December in Breitbrunn, Chiemsee. She is buried in Prien on the Chiemsee		

Bringing Schulwerk to Life
Persons Associated with Orff and Keetman

The following explanatory notes do not attempt to portray the entire professional relevance of every person mentioned. Rather, the purpose here is to provide brief background information for people whose names appear in the text.

Becker-Ehmck, Klaus
Founder of the company Studio 49, starting the production of Orff Instruments in 1949, the year after the start of the Orff Schulwerk broadcast series at the Bavarian Radio.

Bergese, Hans
Musician, composer; assistant of Carl Orff at the Günther-Schule, later his deputy. He was co-author of the first published Schulwerk books (*Elementare Musikübung*) in 1931.

Günther, Dorothee
Diploma as teacher for *Mensendieck* gymnastics, but multitalented with experience as painter; in 1924 she founded the Günther-Schule in Munich ("Training place of the society for free and applied movement"); Carl Orff established the corresponding music training. Her artistic cooperation with Orff included text adaptations in theater projects, stage and costume designs.

Haselbach, Barbara
Dance pedagogue, pupil of Harald Kreutzberg, successor to Hermann Regner as director of the Orff-Institute. Enhancing and restructuring the IOSFS (International Orff-Schulwerk Forum Salzburg) as a hub and organizing it as an exchange center for the national Orff Schulwerk associations all over the world.

Keller, Wilhelm
Composer, music pedagogue; Carl Orff invited Wilhelm Keller in 1962 to come (back) to Salzburg to relieve him as director of the Orff-Schulwerk Information Center and Seminar, which would soon become the Orff Institute. He dedicated himself from the beginning to the adaptation of the Schulwerk ideas to persons with special needs.

Kestenberg, Leo
Pianist, music pedagogue and politician for cultural affairs; he worked from 1918 in the Prussian Ministry for Culture and Education (*Preussisches Kultusministerium*), directing the Music Department of the Institute for Education and Instruction (*Zentralinstitut für Erziehung und Unterricht*). He was in charge of a general reform of the educational system of the state, but he had to leave Germany because of the Nazi Regime. He lived in Tel Aviv and was awarded the first Honorary President of ISME in recognition of his great distinction in music education.

Maendler, Karl
Harpsichord maker; he built the first xylophones for the Günther-Schule.

Murray, Margaret
Studies at the Royal College of Music, London. She translated and adapted the five original German volumes of *Orff-Schulwerk Music for Children* into English. Among other texts by Carl Orff, she translated his autobiographic *Documentation*. Founder of the Orff Society in the United Kingdom in 1964.

Orff, Gertrud (a.k.a. Willert-Orff, Gertrud)
Second wife of Carl Orff (1939–1953); she was a composer and became involved in the development of Orff Schulwerk. She was one of the first music therapists in the German speaking area and she opened the Orff Schulwerk to music therapy for children with special needs, including autistic children. Her lectures and publications brought her international recognition.

Orff, Godela
Carl Orff's daughter from his first marriage (with Alice Solscher); actress, first "Agnes Bernauer" in Orff's opera *Die Bernauerin* (1947), presenter of Orff Schulwerk in a TV program (*Musik für Kinder*) at *Bayerischer Rundfunk* in Munich together with Gunild Keetman from 1957 until 1959.

Orff, Liselotte
Fourth wife and widow of Carl Orff (they married in 1960). After Carl Orff's death in 1982 she became the first president of Carl Orff Foundation, a position she held for 24 years.

Panofsky, Walter
Music journalist cooperating with the Bavarian Radio (*Bayerischer Rundfunk*). He gave a copy of a recording of Orff and Keetman's compositions written for the 1936 Olympic Games to the head of the schools broadcast (Annemarie Schambeck) with the proposal to invite Carl Orff for a series of broadcasts.

Preussner, Eberhard
Music pedagogue, staff member of Leo Kestenberg at the *Zentralinstitut für Erziehung und Unterricht* in Berlin. He facilitated the meeting between Carl Orff and Leo Kestenberg in 1932 (to talk about the possibility of introducing the Schulwerk into Berlin schools). Later he came as professor to the Academy of Music and Performing Arts "Mozarteum" at Salzburg (1959 he became Director). He enabled the start of children's classes taught by Gunild Keetman at the Mozarteum in the autumn of 1949. Thanks to his commitment, the Orff Institute could find its own building next to Schloss Frohnburg. It opened its doors on the 25th of October 1963.

Regner, Hermann
Composer, musicologist, music pedagogue; he followed Wilhelm Keller as director of the Orff Institute. He took special care to develop the international scope of the Orff Institute, but also kept a close relationship to the Bavarian Radio, where the Orff Schulwerk started in 1948. He produced a great number of programs about the Schulwerk on radio and television.

Ronnefeld, Minna
Pianist, music pedagogue, editor and producer of radio programs in Austria and Denmark; assistant and successor to Gunild Keetman for teaching the subject Orff Schulwerk at the Mozarteum College of Music and Performing Arts.

Sachs, Curt

Musicologist, one of the most important scientists for describing and cataloguing musical instruments. At the time of cooperation with Carl Orff he was director of the State Collection of Musical Instruments (*Staatliche Musikinstrumentensammlung*) in Berlin. With the beginning of the Nazi Regime, he had to leave Germany.

Schambeck, Annemarie

From 1945, staff member of the Bavarian state radio station *Bayerischer Rundfunk* (in the first years after the war named Radio München). In 1947 she was assigned to build and direct an educational department at the radio station. With help of Walter Panofsky, she invited Carl Orff to design a radio program that let the listening children actively participate.

Strecker, Ludwig and Willy

Music publishers, sons of Ludwig Strecker (senior), the owners of the publishing house B. Schott's Söhne (today, Schott Music), directing the company after the death of their father in 1943. Close friendship with Carl Orff.

Thomas, Werner

Musicologist, classical philologist; analyzer of Carl Orff's work; adviser and friend of Carl Orff; participated in the documentation of the eight volumes of *Carl Orff and His Work*.

Wigman, Mary

Dancer; after studies with Dalcroze in Dresden she developed her own dance style that became known as "New German Dance." In 1920, she founded her own "Wigman-School." Characteristic of her performances was her way of connecting dance with a rich collection of drums, rattles, recorders. Her *Hexentanz* (dance of the witch) became famous. It was an inspiring step for Carl Orff in developing his form of elemental music.

References

Bluestine, E. (2000). *The Ways Children Learn Music, an Introduction and Practical Guide to Music Learning Theory*. Chicago: GIA Publications.

Brunnhuber, P. (1971). *Prinzipien einer effektiven Unterrichtsgestaltung* [Principles of Effective Teaching]. Donauwörth: Auer.

Gordon Institute for Music Learning. (2021). About Music Learning Theory. https://giml.org/mlt/about/

Günther, D. (2011/1932). The Rhythmic Person and Their Education (M. Murray, Trans.). In B. Haselbach (Ed.). *Texts on Theory and Practice of Orff-Schulwerk: Basic Texts from the Years 1932–2010* (pp. 88–90). Mainz: Schott. (Original work published 1932)

Harding, J. (2013). *From Wibbleton to Wobbleton*. San Francisco: Pentatonic Press.

Hartmann, W. (1989/1984). Can we make up something again today (M. Murray, Trans.). In ORFF TIMES 10(2). Original work published 1984 as "…dürfen wir heute wieder etwas erfinden" Kreative Möglichkeiten im Musikunterricht. In *Musik und Bildung*, 12.

———. (2000). Creative Playgrounds–Music by Children. In A. de Quadros (Ed.), *Many Seeds, Different Flowers— The Music Education Legacy of Carl Orff* (pp. 94–99). Perth: The University of Western Australia, CIRCME.

———, [coop. with B. Haselbach]. (2019, Fall). The Principles of Orff Schulwerk (V. Maschat, Trans.). *The Orff Echo*, 52(1), 8-12.

Haselbach, B., (Ed.). (2011). *Texts on Theory and Practice of Orff-Schulwerk Basic Texts from the Years 1932–2010*. Mainz: Schott.

Haselbach, B., Nykrin, R., & Regner, H., (Eds.). (1996). *Musik und Tanz für Kinder* [Music and Dance for Children]. Mainz: Schott.

Jans, H. J., (Ed.) (1996). *Welttheater Carl Orff und sein Bühnenwerk, Texte von Carl Orff aus der Dokumenation* [World Theater Carl Orff and his Stage Works, Texts by Carl Orff from the Documentation]. Tutzing: Hans Schneider.

Jungmair, U. (1992). *Das Elementare—Zur Musik- und Bewegungserziehung im Sinne Carl Orffs* [The Elemental – Music and Movement Education in the Spirit of Carl Orff]. Mainz: Schott.

———. (1996, Summer). Komponieren wir was [Let's Compose Something]. *Orff-Schulwerk Informationen 56*, 17–25.

Kallós, C., (Ed.). (2004). Musik von Gunild Keetman [Music by Gunild Keetman; DVD in H. Regner & M. Ronnefeld (Eds.), *Gunild Keetman: A Life Given to Music and Movement*]. Mainz: Schott.

Kater, M. (1995). Carl Orff im Dritten Reich [Carl Orff in the Third Reich]. *Vierteljahreshefte für Zeitgeschichte 43(1)*, pp. 1–36. München: Institut für Zeitgeschichte.

Keetman, G. (1974/1970). *Elementaria – First Acquaintance with Orff-Schulwerk* (M. Murray, Trans.). London: Schott. (Original work published 1970)

———. (2011/1978). Memories of the Günther-Schule (M. Murray, Trans.). In B. Haselbach (Ed.), *Texts on Theory and Practice of Orff-Schulwerk Basic Texts from the Years 1932–2010* (pp. 44–64). Mainz: Schott. (Original work published 1978)

Keller, W. (1954). *Einführung in Musik für Kinder–Orff-Schulwerk* [Introduction to Music for Children–Orff-Schulwerk; also available in English translation by S. Kennedy published 1974, Schott Mainz]. Mainz: Schott.

———. (n.d. and 1973–1975). *Ludi Musici–Schall–und Sprachspiele, Spiellieder, miniSPECTACULA* [Ludi Musici –Sound and Speech Games, Play Songs, miniSPECTACULA]. Boppard, Salzburg: Fidula.

Kugler, M. (2000). *Die Methode Jaques–Dalcroze und das Orff-Schulwerk "Elementare Musikübung," bewegungsorientierte Konzeptionen der Musikpädagogik* [The Jaques-Dalcroze Method and the Orff-Schulwerk "Elemental Music," Movement-oriented Conceptions of Music Education]. Frankfurt am Main: Peter Lang, Europäischer Verlag der Wissenschaften.

———. (2011). Introduction (M. Murray, Trans.). In B. Haselbach (Ed.), *Texts on Theory and Practice of Orff-Schulwerk Basic Texts from the Years 1932–2010* (pp. 14–42). Mainz: Schott.

———, (Ed.). (2013/2002). *Elemental Dance–Elemental Music: The Munich Günther School 1924–1944* (M. Murray, Trans.). Mainz: Schott. (Original work published 2002)

———. (2013a/2002). The Path to Elemental Dance and Elemental Music (M. Murray, Trans.). In M. Kugler (Ed.), *Elemental Dance–Elemental Music: The Munich Günther School 1924–1944* (pp. 9–19). Mainz: Schott. (Original work published 2002)

———. (2013b/2002). Hans Bergese. In M. Kugler (Ed.), *Elemental Dance–Elemental Music: The Munich Günther School 1924–1944* (pp. 93–103). Mainz: Schott. (Original work published 2002)

Maier, H. (1995). *Carl Orff in seiner Zeit, Rede anlässlich Carl Orffs 100. Geburtstag München, Prinzregententheater, 7. Juli 1995* [Carl Orff in his Time, Speech on the Occasion of Carl Orff's 100th Birthday Munich, Prinzregententheater, 7 July 1995]. Mainz: Schott.

Maschat, V. (2004). Gunild Keetman and Us Children (M. Murray, Trans.). In H. Regner & M. Ronnefeld (Eds.), *Gunild Keetman 1904–1990: A Life Given to Music and Movement* (pp. 72–76). Mainz: Schott.

O'Hehir, M. M. (2020, Winter). Review of Elementaria by G. Keetman. The Orff Echo, 52(2), 59-60.

Orff, C. (1934a). *Klavierübung, kleines Spielbuch*. Mainz: Schott.

———. (1934b). *Geigenübung I + II*. Mainz: Schott.

———. (1964). Orff-Schulwerk: Rückblick und Ausblick [Orff-Schulwerk: Past and Future]. In W. Thomas & W. Götze (Eds.), *ORFF-INSTITUT Jahrbuch 1963* (pp. 13–20). Mainz: Schott.

———. (1975–1984). *Carl Orff und sein Werk, Dokumentation* [Carl Orff and His Work, Documentation] 7 volumes. Tutzing: Hans Schneider.

———. (1975a). *Carl Orff und sein Werk, Dokumentation: Bd. 1. Erinnerung* [Carl Orff and His Work, Documentation: Vol. 1. Memory]. Tutzing: Hans Schneider.

———. (1975b). *Carl Orff und sein Werk, Dokumentation: Bd. 2. Lehrjahre bei den alten Meistern* [Carl Orff and His Work, Documentation: Vol. 2. Years of Apprenticeship with the Old Masters]. Tutzing: Hans Schneider.

———. (1978/1976). *The Schulwerk* (M. Murray, Trans.). New York: Schott. (Original work published 1976 as Vol. 3 of Carl Orff und sein Werk, Dokumentation: Bd. 3. Das Schulwerk)

———. (2011/1932). Thoughts about Music with Children and Non-professionals (M. Murray, Trans.). In B. Haselbach (Ed.), *Texts on Theory and Practice of Orff-Schulwerk: Basic Texts from the Years 1932–2010* (pp. 66–76). Mainz: Schott. (Original work published 1932)

———. (2011/1964). Orff-Schulwerk: Past & Future. In B. Haselbach (Ed.), *Texts on Theory and Practice of Orff-Schulwerk: Basic Texts from the Years 1932–2010* (pp. 134–156). Mainz: Schott. (Original work published 1964)

———. (2013/1932-33). Elemental Music Practice, Improvisation and Non-professional Training (M. Murray, Trans.). In Kugler, M. (Ed.), *Elemental Dance–Elemental Music: The Munich Günther School 1924–1944* (pp. 158–166). Mainz: Schott. (Original work published 1932-33)

Orff, C., & Keetman, G. (1950–1954). *Orff-Schulwerk, Musik für Kinder* (Vols. 1–5). Mainz: Schott.

———. (1957–1966). *Orff-Schulwerk, Music for Children* (Vols. 1–5) (English adaptation by M. Murray). London: Schott.

Panofsky, W. (1962). Orff-Schulwerk im Radio [Orff-Schulwerk on the Radio]. In W. Thomas & W. Götze (Eds.), *ORRF-INSTITUT Jahrbuch 1962* (pp. 70–73). Mainz: Schott.

Quantz, J. J. (1752). *Versuch einer Anweisung die Flöte traversiere zu spielen*. Reprint (1983). Kassel: Bärenreiter.

Regner, H. (1976). *Chorstudien*. Mainz: Schott.

———, (Ed.). (1977-1982). *Music for Children–Orff-Schulwerk–American Edition*. New York: Schott Music Corp.

———. (1994). *Carl Orff und das Dritte Reich* [Carl Orff and the Third Reich]. Speech manuscript at Orff Zentrum München.

———. (2011/1984). "Musik für Kinder – Music for Children – Musique pour Enfants," Comments on the Adoption and Adaptation of Orff-Schulwerk in Other Countries (M. Murray, Trans.). In B. Haselbach (Ed.), *Texts on Theory and Practice of Orff-Schulwerk Basic Texts from the Years 1932–2010* (pp. 220–244). Mainz: Schott. (Original work published 1984)

Regner, H., & Ronnefeld, M., (Eds.). (2004). *Gunild Keetman 1904–1990: A Life Given to Music and Movement*. Mainz: Schott.

Riveiro Holgado, L. (2007, Summer). Vom Instrumentenbau zur elementaren Komposition–Prinzipien und Fundamente [From Building Instruments to Elemental Composition]. *Orff-Schulwerk Informationen 77*, 18.

Ronnefeld, M. (2013/2002). Gunild Keetman – Pedagogue and Composer (M. Murray, Trans.). In M. Kugler (Ed.), *Elemental Dance–Elemental Music: The Munich Günther School 1924–1944* (pp. 81–92). Mainz: Schott. (Original work published 2002)

———. (2004a). In the workshop with Gunild Keetman (M. Murray, Trans.). In H. Regner & M. Ronnefeld (Eds.), *Gunild Keetman 1904–1990: A Life Given to Music and Movement* (pp. 178–182). Mainz: Schott.

———. (2004b). Gunild Keetman – Fragments of a Life (M. Murray, Trans.). In H. Regner & M. Ronnefeld (Eds.), *Gunild Keetman 1904–1990: A Life Given to Music and Movement* (pp. 14–48). Mainz: Schott.

Rösch, T. (2009). Carl Orff – *Musik zu Shakespeares Ein Sommernachtstraum Entstehung und Deutung* [Music to Shakespeare's *A Midsummer Night's Dream* Origin and Interpretation]. München: Orff-Zentrum.

Seashore, C. E. (1967/1938). *Psychology of music*. New York: Dover Publications. (Original work published 1938)

Stewart, C. (1996, Spring). President's Message. *The Orff Echo, 28*(3), 5–7.

Thomas, W. (1985). In Rootless Times the Deeply Rooted Makes Impact: Orff-Schulwerk Yesterday, Today and Tomorrow (M. Murray, Trans.). In H. Regner (Ed.), *Symposion 1985: Orff-Schulwerk in der Welt von Morgen* [Symposium 1985: Orff-Schulwerk in the World of Tomorrow] (pp. 27–29). Salzburg: Orff Institute.

———. (1986). Carl Orff. In Jahresgabe der Orff-Schulwerk Gesellschft in der Bundesrepublik Deutschland e.V. Weihnachten 1986 [Annual gift of the Orff-Schulwerk Association in the Federal Republic of Germany, Christmas 1986]. Berlin: Propyläen. (Reprinted from L. Gall (Ed.), *Die grossen Deutschen unserer Epoche* [The Great Germans of our Time] (1985)).

———. (1990). *Das Rad der Fortuna* [The Wheel of Fortune]. Mainz: Schott.

———. (2004/1991). Obituary for Gunild Keetmen (M. Murray, Trans.). In H. Regner & M. Ronnefeld (Eds.), *Gunild Keetman 1904–1990: A Life Given to Music and Movement* (pp. 154–160). Mainz: Schott. (Originally published 1991)

———. (1995). *"Ein anderer Carl Orff im Dritten Reich," Reply to Michael H. Kater's article "Carl Orff im Dritten Reich."* Speech manuscript at Orff Zentrum München.

Widmer, M. (2011). *Die Pädagogik des Orff-Instituts* [The Pedagogy of the Orff Institute]. Mainz: Schott.

Wieblitz, E. (1978). Schallerzeugung im Anfang, Instrumente erfinden–bauen–spielen, Improvisation als Prinzip im Unterricht [Sound generation in the beginning, inventing-building-playing instruments, improvisation as a principle in the classroom]. In L. Auerbach, H. W. Köneke, & W. Stumme (Eds), *Musikalische Grundausbildung in der Musikschule, Lehrerhandbuch, Teil 1*. Mainz: Schott.

———. (1987). Komponieren mit Selbstbauinstrumenten [Composing with Self-made Instruments]. *Orff-Schulwerk Informationen 40*, 26–32.

Woodford, P. G. (1996, Fall). Evaluating Edwin Gordon's Music Learning Theory from a Critical Thinking Perspective. In *Philosophy of Music Education Review* 4(2), 83–95.

ABOUT THE AUTHOR

Wolfgang Hartmann studied Pedagogy for Grund- und Hauptschule at the University of Würzburg. After he was granted a State Scholarship from the Bavarian State Government for a study of two years at the Orff Institute (Musikuniversität "Mozarteum") in Salzburg/Austria he taught at two "Orff Modellschulen" (state schools with classes that have extended music lessons) in Munich. At that time, he also began to make music education programs at the radio station *Bayerischer Rundfunk*, the same station where Orff and Keetman presented the Orff Schulwerk. Some broadcasts referred directly to the Schulwerk (*Kinder machen Musik–Neue Wege zum Orff-Schulwerk*).

After moving to Austria, he became director of the Music School at Klagenfurt and a teacher at the Carinthian State Conservatory at Klagenfurt (teacher for Orff Schulwerk and head of the Department for Instrumental and Vocal Pedagogy). While in Carinthia he prepared and performed educational concerts for children with the Carinthian Saxophone Quartet and performed semi-professionally with a trombone quartet. He was also a lecturer at the Music University in Vienna (1992–2005) and a guest teacher at the Orff Institute in Salzburg. He is a Visiting Professor at the Conservatory of Music in Shanghai and at the Central Conservatory of Beijing.

For several years he served as business director in the Carl Orff Foundation during the time that Liselotte Orff was president, and for many years he was on the Board of the International Orff-Schulwerk Forum Salzburg. From 2006 until his retirement in 2019 he was a teacher at the conservatory MUSIKENE (*Centro Superior de Música del País Vasco*) at San Sebastián–Donostia in Spain.

Hartmann has given Orff Schulwerk workshops in more than 30 countries, has written numerous articles about music education and the libretti for two children's operas, a musical, a chamber opera, and many other works. Together with Hermann Regner and Rudolf Nykrin he is co-editor of instrumental pedagogical material at Schott Mainz.

OTHER PENTATONIC PRESS PUBLICATIONS

ORFF SCHULWERK IN DIVERSE CULTURES: An Idea That Went Round the World—Edited by Barbara Haselbach and Carolee Stewart ($20)
A collection of articles by some 70 authors from over 25 countries describing how Orff Schulwerk has evolved in their country and impacted their music education culture. This is Volume II of the series *Texts on Theory and Practice of Orff-Schulwerk* (2011-Schott Pub.) (2021)

TEACH LIKE IT'S MUSIC: An Artful Approach to Education—Doug Goodkin ($20)
A look at some of the details behind inspired teaching, with emphasis on creating a musical flow in one's classes with enticing beginnings, connected middles and satisfying endings. A seamless blend of philosophy, pedagogy and practical ideas useful for teachers of all subjects. (2019)

FROM WIBBLETON TO WOBBLETON: Adventures in the Elements of Music and Movement—James Harding ($30)
Integrated arts lessons with graphic illustrations. Includes arrangements of nursery rhymes for Orff instruments. (2013)

ALL BLUES: Jazz for the Orff Ensemble—Doug Goodkin ($38)
36 pieces including roots, vocal blues and jazz blues scored for Orff Instruments, with accompanying CD of children playing the arrangements. The first of several supplements to Now's the Time. (2012)

BLUE IS THE SEA: Music, Dance & Visual Arts—Sofía López-Ibor ($45)
Integrated arts and activities for preschool, elementary and middle school that includes poetry, dance, drama, artwork in various media and music arranged for Orff Ensemble. Many examples of student art and photos of children, all in full vibrant color. (2011)

INTERY MINTERY: Nursery Rhymes for Body, Voice and Orff Ensemble
—Doug Goodkin ($32)
48 activities connecting music and poetry, with musical scores and suggested lesson plans. (2008)

THE ABC'S OF EDUCATION: A Primer for Schools to Come—Doug Goodkin ($18)
26 essays imagining ways in which schools could be refreshed by including Arts, Beauty, Character and more. (2006)

NOW'S THE TIME: Teaching Jazz to All Ages—Doug Goodkin ($38)
A unique approach to jazz education via Orff practice. 64 activities that move from speech, movement, body percussion and roots music to blues, jazz standards and compositions arranged for Orff instruments. (2004)